ACPL IT ☑ S0-ATG-263
DISCARDED

DO NOT REMOVE
CARDS FROM POCKET

* 617 K86I   7046202
KRAMER, MARK, 1944-
INVASIVE PROCEDURES :

ALLEN COUNTY PUBLIC LIBRARY

FORT WAYNE, INDIANA 46802

You may return this book to any agency, branch,
or bookmobile of the Allen County Public Library.

DEMCO

INVASIVE PROCEDURES

Also by MARK KRAMER

MOTHER WALTER AND THE PIG TRAGEDY

THREE FARMS: *Making Milk, Meat and Money from the American Soil*

INVASIVE PROCEDURES

A year in the world of two surgeons

———

Mark Kramer

1817

HARPER & ROW, PUBLISHERS, New York
Cambridge, Philadelphia, San Francisco,
London, Mexico City, São Paulo, Sydney

ALLEN COUNTY PUBLIC LIBRARY
FORT WAYNE, INDIANA

To Dinah and William,
Mildred and Louis,
Esther and Sidney

Portions of this work originally appeared in *Atlantic Monthly*.

A few pages of Chapter 5 contain material, used with permission of the publisher, from Henry Wechsler's *Handbook of Medical Specialties*, copyright © 1976, Human Sciences Press, New York.

INVASIVE PROCEDURES. Copyright © 1979, 1983 by Mark Kramer. All rights reserved. Printed in the United States of America. No part of this book may be used or reproduced in any manner whatsoever without written permission except in the case of brief quotations embodied in critical articles and reviews. For information address Harper & Row, Publishers, Inc., 10 East 53rd Street, New York, N.Y. 10022. Published simultaneously in Canada by Fitzhenry & Whiteside Limited, Toronto.

FIRST EDITION

Designer: C. Linda Dingler

Library of Congress Cataloging in Publication Data

Kramer, Mark, 1944–
    Invasive procedures.

    1. Surgery—Practice—United States.   2. Surgeons—
United States.   3. Surgery—Patients—United States—
Psychology.   I. Title.
RD27.42.K73   1983   617′.0973   82-48672
ISBN 0-06-015160-9

---

83 84 85 86 87 10 9 8 7 6 5 4 3 2 1

7046202

Contents

Acknowledgments

Both of the surgeons who are my subjects were kind enough at the beginning of our work together to sign releases that have allowed me to write forthrightly about them. I acknowledge great debts of gratitude to both of them, and to their families, for frankness and generosity with time, information, and shared access.

I also extend warm thanks to: My editors, Dick Todd of *Atlantic Monthly*, who set me to it, and Ted Solotaroff of Harper & Row, who saw me through it. Roberta Berrien, who narrowed things down until they opened up, and Ed Manwell, Paul Friedmann, Terry Maloney, Hal Strelnick, Mark Gilbert, and Gerson Lesser, who helped explain exotic events. The distinguished social scientists Renee Fox and John Erenreich, who shared key work and insight. Professors Don Robinson, Andy Zimbalist, Sinan Koont, Jill Conway, Joan Berzoff, David Lynch, Ned DeLaCour, Martha Fowkes, and Peter Rose, and John LaGreze, Wendy Posner, Ed and Jane Pincus, Tony Bell, Kirsten McInnis, Jan Wojcik, Peter Wernick, Ruth and Morris Pottish, Rebecca Anwar, Edwin Reubens, Barbara Stack, Temma Kaplan, Howard Higman, Hank Bennett, Noel Perrin, Lynn Kippax, Judith Maloney, Bob Miller, Barbara Shamblin, Dinah Lipman, and Sandy Terry, for providing shelter, insight, and counsel. Deborah Robson, who decoded and copy-edited cryptographic manuscript incisively, and Judy Bauer and Kay Worsley, who made sense of my muttered requests and went one better. My writing students at Smith College, who insisted that I get things right even when I was distracted. The Ford Foundation (and Dick Sharpe) for the award of funds in support of this book. The many doctors, nurses, surgical technicians, hospital administrators, and other health personnel who shared their experience and elected to do so quietly. The patients who all permitted me to witness their excursions into surgeons' territory. And finally, two aggregates, Apple Corps and the Bay State Writers' Collaborative. The book's virtues are built on the generosity of these people; its failings are my own.

INVASIVE PROCEDURES

Invasive Procedures is factually accurate, except that names have been changed and locales and individual traits have been altered where necessary.

Prologue

When I was twenty-three, a bump crawled onto my hip. One day it wasn't there, I'm sure. The next it was. I looked down and it had come—the surfaced knuckle of some buried fist, mimicking the tip of the pelvic bone an inch away. It signaled corruption, through and through, of the body I'd inhabited without suspicion until the moment before. I went to a doctor just off Fifth Avenue, whose office door opened only after negotiation by intercom.

"Who did you say?"

I shouted my name a second time.

"Delivery or appointment?"

"What?"

The door buzzed. Eventually, the doctor saw me.

He said, "This bump troubles me." I signed into the hospital the next day. It was a Friday. One should begin hospital stays on Monday mornings. I'd been declared officially sick, but for days they didn't do anything to me; things slow up for weekends. I felt as well as I had the week before, except more worried. I had been working as a journalist. I carried on from my cranked-up bed, with a portable typewriter propped on my knees, and it felt a little bit heroic.

You're supposed to eagerly conform to all doctors' orders

because you want to do whatever you can to get better and get back to the office. I wanted to deny that I was sick, that I needed the hospital and the doctors. So I bridled at regulations. I wouldn't stay put. Sunday afternoon I wandered off in my bathrobe on an excursion to the farthest wings of the hospital while, it turned out, nurses were hunting for me so they could send me to X-ray. "Where have *you* been?" one said when I finally showed up in my room, where my supper tray was already cooling on the bed table. The nurse said, "We're responsible for you." I'm sure my answer was vague, and I later was to wonder if it had cost me, in slowed postsurgical bedpan service.

All weekend and Monday too, when normal people were off at work, I took long languid baths, two a day, in milky disinfectant, cleansing myself in preparation for the surgeon. Monday afternoon, an orderly with a green wheelchair strode in and said he was to transport me to X-ray—the trip I'd missed the day before. I got in. Then I stepped back out. I folded my arms across my chest and refused to move. I told the man I'd just been all over on foot, and they hadn't done anything yet to slow me down except feed me hospital food. The man stood behind the green wheelchair and reasoned, with surprising patience and understanding, about insurance, his orders, usual procedure, this had never happened to him before, he only worked here. Then he called the head nurse, and she came and went away and came back again with a handsome doctor, young but white-haired, whose blue eyes read me and transmitted his contempt. He just shook his head, but I felt my cheeks redden. I was awed by his detachment, by his authority as a doctor. Suddenly, I knew how very scared I was of the bump, and I thought he must know it too. I needed him and his colleagues. I buckled. I felt sick. I rode down to X-ray, cowed. Once back in my room, I felt fury—not about hospital routine now, but about being ill. My surgeon visited for a moment that evening. He turned out to be short and swarthy, and he had a little neat pompadour combed into his hair. He'd heard about me and the wheelchair. He had a cheerful manner. He kidded me about the folly of resisting the will of nurses, then left.

2

That night I experimented with holding the absolute knowledge that I was fatally ill: "Cancer has invaded my bones and life has been short and has served little purpose." Then I'd haul myself out of self-pity and experiment with the absolute knowledge that I was well, that this was a mistake, just me being too worried, or that it wasn't me at all, or that the odds I'd been quoted by the surgeon: "Eighty percent chance it's nothing," were so strong that a little scary experience would do me good, purify the spirit. On the strength of that certainty I'd go back to the typewriter for half an hour and then grow afraid again.

At ten or eleven at night, a nurse's aide, a Haitian with reddened eyes, a loping island accent, and a gleeful laugh, befriended me. My college French was not up to her explanations about her family and children back home. A nurse sent her away and gave me a sleeping pill. I found myself fighting it for hours until it wore off. The Haitian aide came back in the middle of the night, closed the door to my room, and shared vodka and orange juice with me. Home in the midst of despair, I finally slept.

The surgeon stopped by again, shortly after dawn. He was paunchy, jolly in the day as well as the night, and so recently shaved that his chin shone slate-blue. He told me numbers— boring details of incredible interest to me. Two hours or so in surgery. Four hours in the recovery room. Ten more days in the hospital, gathering strength. Verdict as soon as I woke up. By the way, did I play basketball? I remember feeling a moment's love for him then. I was very interested in him. He was about to get to know me intimately.

A few minutes later, an olive-drab anesthesiologist with an Indian accent came by, guessed my weight to within five pounds, and asked about allergies. I slept again, awakened, scared, and was sucking on a Marlboro, my last, desperate, cigarette of a lifetime, when a huge black male nurse, as bald and muscular as Mr. Clean, stuck me with a sedative. I lost what little will I had left.

I recall, I think, lying on the cart, inside what must have been the surgical corridor, surprised that everyone ran around in pastel-blue scrubsuits. I was free of choices, adrift in their hands. In a moment of inane surprise, I noticed another young man parked next to me, staring back, then asleep.

I'm quite sure I remember the coolness of the draping sheets as they hauled me from the cart onto the table. And I awakened, for just one minute, in the recovery room, with the surgeon jiggling a tube that ran into my nose, and shouting, "Not cancer."

Moments or hours before or after that, someone adjusted the tube in the nose again. I can recreate the gritty intracranial tugging. And still later, the surgeon leaned over and quietly said he'd taken away a small block of hip, then had flared the edge of the remaining bone, "so your pants will hang on you, and not fall down." A joke. He told me he'd done a beautiful job. I took heart from the evidence that he was thinking of my future. I slept all day and knew even when I slept that I hurt.

The next day, my family, and a few nurses, told me things had gone well. I didn't believe them. The pain was far stronger than any I'd ever experienced. Now I can't remember what it felt like at all, but I have known during my few other moments of pain that nothing compared to the power of the hurting hip the day after surgery.

Under morphine, I dreamed obsessively of a broad living room, where each piece of furniture stood far from every other, and whose cantilevered beams were laminated of cement and pain. Every beam had a name and the names were secret. A girl in Russian peasant clothes, a tiny figure at the far end of the room, danced a kazatsky. She was bald, alabaster-headed; features had been drawn on her face in India ink. It doesn't make sense now, but at the time it was my world—far more reasonable and consuming than the momentary chats with hospital visitors.

On the third evening after surgery, a friend showed up, on his way to work, carrying a banjo case. I paid attention. He made me laugh so much I cried in pain and had to ask him not to say anything. Then we got the agonizing giggles, like school-boys under discipline. That night, the pain dulled and I came fully to my senses. For the first time I looked around the bland

4

room and took note of gray pebble-grained wallpaper and a nice view of the city. I knew that in my infidel way, I was born again. General anesthesia sends the soul off. It had inserted what I then took to be an experienceless time, a blank space, into my life. It had rendered my being, which had been continuous since childhood, discontinuous—on, then off, then turned back on again, this one time at least.

The Haitian nurse's aide showed up again on the late shift. She sat on my bed, smelling of musky rose, sweeping wax, and alcohol, and beamed at me in the dim night-light. I eased myself up in bed, a few inches. She stroked my cheek.

"Well, *petit monsieur*, you are not feeling all so good tonight?"

"Better than yesterday, thank you."

"And what is the result?"

"They say it was a benign thing—nothing—that grew there and now they've taken it away."

"*Est-ce-que tu peux les croire?*" she asked, smiling still—can you believe them?

"I think I do."

"Surgeons never tell the truth. They tell what makes it easy for themselves." She spoke dramatically, in a breathy whisper.

It took me a day to understand how devastating she'd been, and during that day I homed in on bitter lines from John Donne's "Noctourne upon St. Lucie's Day":

Study me then, you who shall lovers be
At the next world, that is, at the next spring:
 For I am every dead thing . . .
He ruined me, and I am re-begot
Of absence, darkness, death; things which are not.

Bandaged and invaded, robbed of my bone, I felt a kinship with Donne, who had written those lines dressed up in his shroud. I sided with the dead against the living. We dead are an ignored minority. We have our plight too. It seemed like a reasonable position.

Later, as I recovered strength, I came up with a mundane

axiom: The body leads the mind. My trust, my spirit, curiosity, and affection slowly grew as I healed. After I had been home for a few months, I invited one of the nurses out to supper and watched her carefully over the antipasto to see if she acted as if she were visiting with a dead man. I felt reassured.

Still, life had become odd. I went back to work, but I was like a child who, having thought about how he walks, now stumbled at every step. I let things fall apart. After a few more months I was gone from New York, and was writing newspaper columns from a farm in the New England hills. The surgeon who had operated on me was vacationing in the area and he came by to visit. After lunch, I told him how disorienting my hospitalization had been, but he said that what went on in the hospital didn't have much to do with him. I couldn't understand his feelings, so detached from the effects of his work. We changed the subject and talked farming, and some about basketball.

———————

Fifteen years later, my curiosity about surgery is again stirred, first by an experimental psychologist at a loud party. He has a long beard and his eye glitters. He urges me to hear him out, guiding me with his skinny hand to a bench. He shouts over the bass thump of a rock record. He knows something that ought to change how surgeons work. It's important; there are over fifteen million surgical procedures performed in America under general anesthesia every year. No one wants to listen and don't I write? Have I ever had surgery?

He's just done a postdoctoral research year at a big teaching hospital. He put microphones into the ears of anesthetized patients and recorded what they'd hear if they were awake. "They *do* hear what happens. Most anesthetics don't block hearing, they just set up deep postsurgical amnesia. Surgical patients take in what's happening, react to it, even heal better or worse according to what's said by surgeons and nurses who think patients are out cold. There's a small but convincing body of experimen-

6

tal data. I added my own few experiments.

"I whispered in patients' ears that a week from now, an interviewer in a red shirt will ask them about how their surgery had gone, and it is very important to the doctor that they then pull on one of their ears. They were supposedly asleep. Their bellies or chests were opened right up. A week after each one's operation, I had a student in a red shirt interview each of fifty surgical patients—only half of whom had had the ear-pulling suggestion. The student didn't know who was who. It was remarkable. The group I'd whispered to tugged away at their ears—nine times as often as the other group. They'd heard. Their egos were demolished and that's the state they were in when they'd heard. How do you think patients react inside when their surgeons joke about their being old or ugly or fat or crazy, or being disaster cases? What happens to the anesthetized patient who takes in the words of some powerful surgeon saying, 'This one's a mess. He won't last a week'?"

I wonder, as I free myself from the grasp of this man, what my own surgeon might have said while operating, fifteen years before, upon a panicky young man who was overreacting to a routine and only somewhat suspicious bump on his hip. Had things he'd said then stayed with me? The operation, late in the sixties, came at a time when I was—in keeping with the time—resistant to authority. Yet I'd quickly become as docile as the old men who had shared the hospital room next door. I'd been trained young to this compliance. The power of doctors interested me; that strong pain had impressed me; and the dislocation and subsequent redefinition of body and being, of course, still concerned me—nothing since has affected me so suddenly and profoundly as the work of that surgeon. The conversation at the loud party reopened a closed topic and a few weeks later I was making plans to visit—to return, in a sense—to see, to touch and try to understand whatever had cut me open and moved me out of town.

1

"It's Considered Bad Form
to Nick the Colon"

"I like to be mean when I operate. I never eat breakfast when I'm operating in the morning," Danny Andersson growls, "and today I feel mean. We're on for two this morning—an amp and an aorta." It's spring. I've gotten myself invited into the operating room, awake this time. We undress in the small gray locker room off the long surgical corridor of his hospital, in the thick of a factory town an hour or two from Boston. It's not long past dawn. We clothe ourselves for action in crepe-paper booties, green pajama bottoms that we both tie up the front, sporty V-necked shirts with short sleeves, and tight cotton surgical caps. I put mine on backward so I can tie the ties in front, then spin it halfway around so that it looks the same as Andersson's.

It's been surprisingly easy to enter this sanctum. There are two ways in, and the second one has worked. You can go to the public relations office of a hospital large enough to have one and state your business, goals, research aims, and affiliations, and eventually, after administrative brooding, they will tell you they are terribly sorry, but patients' rights to privacy must be protected, and insurance considerations prevent favorable response, and it's medically irresponsible to incur extraneous sources of contamination in the operating room, but that they would be happy to help you in any way they can.

Or you can go to an established, influential senior surgeon who is a friend of a friend and say you want to see him work, and why. I went to Danny Andersson. I told him I wanted to understand, by paying attention to the people involved, some of the effects of some of the social, political, commercial, and technical changes in surgery, and that ultimately I was interested in how power works in his world. He said that he would be fascinated to see how an outsider regarded such things in his life. He'd arrange everything. He'd even sign a release, allowing me to write freely about him. And he did.

My new guide is a vascular surgeon in his late forties, a rangy man of optimistic nature. He flashes sudden sunbeam smiles, then holds them and looks into my eyes until I offer some sign that these offerings have been appreciated. I find myself nodding at him a lot. His family has been here for generations, he explains to me, especially on his mother's side—DAR, in fact—so I shouldn't be thrown off by his Scandinavian name. He is mostly English, even if he is six foot one and has had blond hair. Only a relic of the hair remains, a closely cropped tonsure the color of ash.

As I look around the operating room, at the aqua tiled walls and shining equipment, and at the old man who lies on the operating table, I experiment, briefly, with pretending I am a surgeon. But it's difficult to do, even for a moment, because I don't know what comes next. I'm not looking forward to this first morning in surgery. I turn away during the violent scenes at the movies. Andersson has carried in with him a chrome-stripped portable tape deck and radio with big round speakers, large and flashy enough to outfit any jiving teenager on the streets of Boston. A nurse takes the radio from him and sets it up on a stool of its own in a far corner. The Fourth Brandenburg plays quietly. I watch the preparations through fog. My glasses steam. Andersson, a cordial host, notices. "Pinch the wire nosepiece of the surgical mask so it conforms better to your face," he says.

Nurses, a whistling anesthesiologist, and a beefy surgical resident prepare the man on the table. His name is Luskin. He's diabetic, seventy-one, a former farmhand, a hermit, a bachelor, a security guard with one artificial leg. In Danny Andersson's office three days earlier, he had lurched in past the other patients, barely able to stagger from waiting room to examination room. Andersson had to lift the old man onto the table. The man had stunk—and when Andersson had peeled off the man's white cotton sock he had seen that the odor of decay came from a checker-sized patch of black gangrene on the remaining big toe. Andersson had touched the blotchy leg, run his hand up and down it, feeling for pulses that weren't there.

"It's frank gangrene, Mr. Luskin. I'm probably going to have to take it off."

"The toe."

"We'll see, but I think the leg. The toe wouldn't heal."

After a long silence, Mr. Luskin had said, "I don't like that."

Andersson, satisfied with the preparations, steps out of the room to the stainless steel scrub sink in the middle of the surgical corridor. He peels open a prepackaged scrub set—sterile soap and an abrasive pad—commencing a ritual of his trade.

As he soaps and rinses his hands again and again, I ask him, "What are you going to do?"

"I'm going to make him shorter."

Andersson reenters the operating room like Lady Macbeth the morning after, hands held aloft in front of him. Doreen, a private surgical technician who works for him, stretches sterile gloves over the hands. She smiles. Smiles around here show over the masks, around the eyes.

"We've got half an hour on the schedule. Let's keep it moving." Andersson's white eyebrows are his most prominent feature. Mr. Luskin's eyes are taped shut now, "to keep them from drying out," the anesthesiologist explains. The modern operating table is cruciform; armrests extend from it at right angles. This keeps the arms out of the action, and offers the

10

wrists. Masked, a nurse and the surgical resident work rapidly, binding Mr. Luskin's hands to the table, palms up, then installing long intravenous spikes in both wrists. Another nurse takes a swab and polishes the man orange from the waist down until he glistens.

Three days of antibiotics have taken the fury out of his infection. He breathes in anesthesia. His leg looks pretty. It is hairless, sturdy, the muscles well articulated. It seems horrifying to take off a leg like this.

"The leg is full of dead flesh. I'd like to do a BK—a below-the-knee amp, because then it's easier to use an artificial limb, and easier to hike yourself onto a bedpan. There's some odds playing. A BK heals only 95 percent of the time. We'll tell by blood supply and edema if we have a shot. When I'm going to do an amp, I expect big psychological effects. In the days before the operation I like to let them have so much pain they are glad to get rid of it. Otherwise, no matter how good a job you do, they'll be unhappy about it, wonder if it really had to go. If there's a family, I get them involved in efforts to save the leg. That way, when it goes, everybody gets involved with aftercare, and retraining too." Taking scalpel in hand, Andersson says, "To know the surgeon, you have to start with the surgery."

When it is the next thing to do, he simply slices into the flesh, rings the shin, and heads on down through calf muscle. When I ask, he says the first cut doesn't seem of special moment to him. The incision, surprisingly, turns out to be nearly blood-less. Atherosclerotic deposits already block most circulation to this leg. I am relieved. Whatever does bleed he quickly clamps, sutures, cauterizes. After cutting down until he has rounded the two leg bones, he turns the incision parallel to the table and continues toward the toes for six more inches. Then he completes the circle, leaving a "longitudinal flap" of calf muscle attached to the upper leg stump. He saws through the bone— fourteen strokes for the tibia, by hand, just like a carpenter. Two or three more for the fibula.

"I hate amps," says the circulating nurse, holding her ears against the noise of the sawing. The parted leg comes away. A

11

nurse ties a tag to its great toe, wraps the limb in a plastic sack, and wheels it out of the room on a cart. It seems normal, here, that such a thing should happen to a leg.

The steps a surgeon takes are as orderly, as procedural, as physically explicable, as the steps of disassembling an engine. Step follows step. Twenty minutes after beginning, Andersson is ready to close. The stump looks like soupbone, the longitudinal flap like London broil; the resemblance to food is exact, unavoidable.

Andersson folds the flap upward until its end meets the top of the knee. Then he sews the flap into place with big black lockstitches. The buttock, tinted leg, and sewn stump together resemble a large moccasin. He sews like a bored shoemaker, quickly, exactly, automatically, talking about other things.

"I like operating to Bach. I always have music when I operate. In Vietnam, I welded earphones inside my helmet. Music relieves the tension. I can operate all day. What makes me feel great is operations lined up back-to-back. I go in there and bang, bang, bang."

———————————

Today's a day things are scheduled as he likes them—bang, bang, bang. In the doctors' lounge next to the dressing room, he chats on the phone to his office. He calls the patient's sister and says, "Things went very well." He steps out of his sullied surgical greens and into a clean pair. Surgeons dress and undress all day long. He scrubs his hands elaborately again. Then he enters the operating room next down the corridor, moving from mayhem to mayhem, seemingly taking no more notice of his feelings than a bus driver might take when starting his second route of the day. The room looks like the last one—small, tiled, shined. Three nurses are just putting the final tucks on the draping of this patient. Soon, a green mound, the green of the papier-mâché in a fruit carton, occupies the center of the room. The drapes on the operating table have the contour of a chain of old mountains. No hint of what lies underneath: it could be a goat, or a large sheep. The face is draped too, like the face of some veiled Moslem bride, hooded in tribute to its power to contaminate. The surgery will be an exercise performed upon some abstract sick creature, not on anyone in particular. Andersson, assisted by the resident—who is a surgeon in training—never refers to the patient, but only to the parts encountered and to the shining spreaders, rakes, clamps, and knives he calls for and wields.

"Into the peritoneum, carefully," Andersson says enthusiastically, in a whispery, controlled voice, as he starts this one, "because it's considered bad form to nick the colon." Another innocuous first cut, and then they advance ever deeper, constructing a meat-walled triangular cleft leading in through skin, fat, and muscle, into the belly. They say little as they work; they know the moves. This part of surgery must be standard, the beginning of many abdominal excursions. When the incision easily accommodates the doctors' four hands, two scrub nurses—called that because, like the surgeons, they "scrub in" and don gloves—move up to the table, one on either side, grasp the molded handles of hoe-like retractors, and tug back gently, drawing apart the sides of the opening. Andersson tells me that, unlike most surgeons, he is so busy he has hired his own operating technician, Doreen O'Leary. Andersson introduces her as he cuts.

"How do you do?" she says, holding out a scissors to Andersson. She is wide and sturdy, and even though she stands on a low stool at his right hand, as she does during his every procedure, day or night, the top of her head is below Andersson's shoulder. She is at work, choosing and handing on equipment from the three steel tool tables, each the size of a newspaper page, fanned out to her side. On the tables she has arranged fifty pairs of clamps, decks of sheathed needles prethreaded at the factory, specimen jars, spare aspirators, stacked scissors, pliers, tubes, tongs, tweezers, and scoops, all set out by her idiosyncratically and with the geometric splendor of Hoffritz Cutlery advertisements in *The New York Times*.

Through the slit in the drapes, the reddened wound walls

gleam with clamps that dangle like roots from the sides of a newly dug trench. Andersson expands the incision in stages, cutting, then pausing to clamp "bleeders." He stops whenever a dozen or so of the clamps, called hemostats, have accumulated, and throws stitches over the handles of each. Then he slides each stitch down, and tightens it off the front tip of the clamp. Finally he removes the clamps, and hands them back to Doreen. He throws stitches and clears off clamps very quickly. Doreen is the flywheel in his work, keeping ahead of sporadic heavy demand by placing orders for more tools. Doreen's orders are received by the circulating nurse, the only ungloved nurse in the room, who moves back and forth between the glass-fronted supply cabinets on the walls, and the edge of the sterile operating field. She peels open the packets of needles and the towels full of sterilized clamps she brings to Doreen, holding them away from herself and never touching the contents. Doreen plucks the equipment out, her glove stained with blood.

"If Doreen hands me something I haven't requested," Andersson says, "I think twice, because it's probably just the thing I need."

Doreen beams. "You've seen my true self," she says later.

There's little quipping this day—perhaps because of the newness of my intrusion into a roomful of medical confederates. Andersson's portable tape deck is in here now, retuned to easy listening. As he cuts, clamps, and knots, a thousand fiddle bows slither through the sterile field. Paralyzed by a curare-like muscle relaxant, the patient breathes with the help of an artificial lung that hisses and groans above the draped head, out of pulse with the music.

The spectacle of surgery seems graceful to me, and that impression will remain even as my comprehension of what's taking place grows through a hundred procedures to come. The seven persons working on the incision all move with stressed, directed gestures. Forearms, instruments, gazes—jeweler's lenses protrude like bug eyes from Andersson's operating glasses—all aim into the depth of the wound to the moment's work.

They complete the excursion into the belly. Andersson says,

"I'll run the colon." He slips his hand along the entire length of the gleaming intestines, as if tracing rope through a tangle, and ends up with his arm inside the opening, up to the elbow. "The gut's healthy enough. That's it for the muck-around-ectomy."

He lifts aside the intestines, cradling them in dampened gauze, places the hoe blades of the retractors gently against them, and turns them over to the charge of nurses. What he exposes by drawing away the gut amazes me. Passing down through the wall of the diaphragm, which separates chest from belly, the aorta runs parallel to the spine. Just above the groin, it splits, at the "aortic saddle," into the two iliac arteries that lead on to the femoral arteries of the legs. Andersson has revealed here a pulsing aorta, distended in two places into thin membranous bubbles.

He calls me closer to the wound to peer in at this barely contained dumbbell of blood that shouldn't be there. It matches the X-ray that glows on the light screen hanging on the wall beyond the table. The ancients, feeling through the abdominal wall the strong pulses of blood that bound through aortic aneurysms, theorized that some worthies developed second hearts in their bellies. Andersson's teachers once spiraled silver wire along the inner walls of aneurysms, banding them to encourage clotting. Only in the past few years has a good remedy become available—a graft, a section of aorta woven of Dacron.

Doreen lifts one out of a sterile package the circulating nurse offers her. Andersson lays it over the wound, trims it to size, and hands it back. Dangling, it looks like the torso of a little man in a cummerbund. It's a fat tube, ribbed like vacuum cleaner hose, bifurcating into smaller ribbed tubes, aorta into iliacs. Doreen sucks up a puddle of the patient's blood with a sterilized turkey baster. "They have one in the surgical tool catalogue for twenty bucks, but it's the same as you get at the hardware store for a buck and a quarter, so I buy them there, then autoclave them—same thing with files," Andersson says. Doreen squirts the blood into a stainless steel tray, tosses in the white graft, and swishes it around.

"It must soak, clot. Then when we put it in we run more

blood through it, clamp it at both ends so it will clot there some more, and flush it out, before finally attaching the lower end. That way it doesn't seep much. Eventually, the blood passing through it will form a new lining, a 'neointima,' a living thing almost as good as the lining of a healthy vessel." The famous surgeon Denton Cooley is reported to have once consoled a patient by telling him his Dacron aorta would still be pristine and intact in a thousand years.

Nowadays, installing an aortic graft is institutionalized audacity, a routine stroll on the tightrope. Andersson does this operation sixty times a year. The recipe for the surgery is the same in all cases—it is the same, in fact, for any surgery. Incise, control the blood flow, do your work, close it up and go away. Controlling the blood flow into and out of the body's main artery entails, surprisingly, less work than for some lesser arterial surgery. Still, there is a lot to do, repeatedly exposing, then temporarily clamping off, branching vessels. It takes nearly an hour to organize for one moment.

Many long strands of stretchy tubing, a modern plastic sort that glides around tissue instead of bunching it when drawn past, loop around blood vessels to valve off flow. Andersson runs dozens of red-tinted strands out of the red incision and secures them by clips to the surgical drapes. I think of the binding of Gulliver in Lilliput. The largest lesser vessels, and the aorta and iliacs themselves, he controls not with these bands but with small clamps called mosquitoes and bulldogs.

As he tightens down on them, bloodflow through the aorta to the legs ceases. The quivering aorta is still. The dumbbell has stopped pulsing.

"Now," Andersson says, as if ordering himself to go ahead with what he is about to do. He points a tiny scalpel at the lower bubble, then flicks his wrist downward an inch. A little flower of red blood surrounds the knife, then dissolves. The aorta deflates. Andersson slices down its flabby front wall, opening it up like a hot dog bun. The patient has no aorta. Andersson is now in the patient as far as he can go.

It's no accident that operations are referred to as "invasive

16

procedures." "My surgery is a creative act," Andersson says. "The guy who's doing a good job is putting a part of himself into every patient he operates on." Like many in his profession, he calls his commitment to surgery a "second marriage." He has never taken his wife in to see him working at surgery. But when his elder son reached adolescence, he did bring the boy around.

He takes the reddened graft from the pan where it has been clotting, and begins to sew the fat top end into the trunk of the aorta.

"Not very good tissue here. Like stitching into wet toilet paper," says Andersson. The resident does half the stitches, and after a few minutes gets tangled up.

"If it's not easy, you're not doing it right," Andersson says, "so try using the other hand when you're working back there."

The list of steps needed to reassemble the patient is a long one. It takes several hours more to accomplish. Andersson fills the graft, attached at the top, but clamped off and flopping loosely at the bottom. While it clots again, he moves down the body, peeling back drapes, and opens two disconnected slits, one below each inguinal crease, where right and left legs attach to the trunk. He works down into them in turn, exposing and displaying the femoral arteries. He controls their vascular fields in turn, then flays open both arteries and cleans out the plugs of waxy plaque that have built up where the graft legs will attach. Finally, he flushes out the graft, then tunnels its legs down below the intervening flesh and up into the femoral incisions, and slowly stitches in the graft legs. He unclamps. The graft is complete, a headless homunculus pulsing inside the veiled patient.

"Here's what Ponce de León was searching for," Andersson says, pointing to a wire of blood that squirts upward through a needle hole at the top of the graft. It takes half an hour to track down leaks and stitch them with filaments of thread. He closes the two leg incisions. He releases the intestines (the nurses, yielding up their retractor handles, look relieved), and runs them once again. He folds the wad of yellow fat comprising the potbelly back down into place, which seems a shame. He stitches closed the inner wall of the intestinal sac, and the supporting

17

tissue. He stitches closed the subcutaneous fat. He stitches closed the incision, finally, with coarse black twine.

When I had met Andersson before this day in surgery, he had seemed aloof from the world, affectedly genial, self-absorbed, and masking pride with a measured affability. In surgery, Andersson starts to make sense. In here, tensed, single-minded, and happy, he becomes graceful. It's like hearing a man with a Hungarian accent begin to speak Hungarian. Surgery is simpler than everyday life. Its goals are clear and accomplished with handiwork, with restraint of feeling. The very best one can do is what's required here, even if it may not be enough. And the end is always in sight.

"Skin to skin," as Andersson puts it, it's been a long haul. And at the end comes a miraculous instant, soon after the last stitch of the procedure has been tied off. The nurses face away and peel off their rubber gloves. Andersson packs up his big radio. The anesthesiologist undrapes the patient's head, untapes the eyes, turns off the anesthesia, keeping just the hissing oxygen flowing.

The old man on the table—it turns out to be a man—groans. One nurse turns back and shouts his formal name: "Mr. Lazarus! Mr. Lazarus!" we'll say. It's as if he has freshly arrived, wounded, from somewhere else. I recall a newspaper article from my childhood, reporting that a carpenter had plunged through a hospital skylight he was repairing, landing on an operating table, where surgeons mended his wounds. The patient groans out a word now.

"Yes."

Andersson looks up, smiles, and, carrying the radio, leaves the aqua room. Walking away, down the corridor, he peels the cap from his bald head and says, "I like surgery. There's no other time like it in my life. I go in there knowing that whatever happens is on me, and I don't always know what will happen. At times I'm scared, frightened, back against the wall. I go in there petrified sometimes. But if you're good, things usually go well. There's no feeling like it. If you're not good, you shouldn't be there."

18

Danny Andersson is a man who has created for himself an opportunity, rare nowadays, and the more to be savored for its rarity. He is one of the people who still get to do useful things, one after another. "I'm as happy as a pig in muck," he says to me as we leave the drowsing and shortened Mr. Luskin and the replumbed and still groaning Mr. Lazarus in the recovery room, and dress once more in civilian clothes. "In the middle of the night, when I get a call from another doctor—'Hey, Danny, I've got this ruptured aneurysm here'—I'm wide awake. A fire horse. Someone's going to *die* if I can't help them. *I need you* is the most important thing anyone can hear." More than the chance to perfect a delicate and interesting craft, more than the power, acclaim, deference, affection, even more than the money, he gives me to understand, the idea of being essential is what pleases Andersson.

He takes me home with him. He lives with his wife and three children in lavish countrified comfort a few miles from the hospital. He points, as we drive up, to a grassy, convex hilltop of several acres, rising behind his white house, and tells me he mows the whole thing himself each Saturday morning, riding on his garden tractor, which he also points out to me. He says that except during a few lengthy vacations—during which he plays eighteen holes of golf before breakfast, and another eighteen after lunch—he seldom finds free time. "I think on the tractor," he says.

Weekdays he works from six in the morning until seven each night, then, before turning in, goes back to the hospital for a quick evening round. "If you're not a mother hen, you're not a good doctor," he says. He does most of his medical reading at home after supper, sitting with his wife in the den. He works through stacks of articles, wearing his stereo earphones. He shows me the den and the earphones. He collects antique clocks. He likes Oriental rugs. He does photography. We go to the cellar to see his darkroom. The home is airy, the gardens beauti-

19

ul through the paned windows of the den.

"The music helps me concentrate. It's considered bad form around here if Amy says something to me and I don't hear it." He echoes himself. "Doctors do marry twice—once to their profession. I'm busy, but sometimes I find my way home for lunch, and occasionally I clear whole evenings for the children."

The civic life he describes is built around a rather proprietary interest in the institutions of his town. He is on the board of a bank. He heads the board of a prestigious prep school located down the road from his home. He turns over the fees from his directors' meetings to a lecture series he has endowed at the school. He brings culture to the hinterland. He seems to feel a strong sense of noblesse oblige, and has become a reliable, constant, and principal supporter of local causes, drives, churches, and emergency situations. He made a fifty-dollar contribution to the town ambulance service after they had tried to save the father of a friend of his, whose heart had given out. He was once coach of a Little League team and chairman of the board of the neighborhood Congregational church. He has settled where a seignorial role can be his; I suspect his pleasure in being necessary has led him to shape an exemplary life just out of range of the grand Boston medical establishment.

We eat supper, we chat—no earphones tonight—until after ten. Andersson and his wife retire, speaking confidentially as they go upstairs. I finish my drink and head for the guest room. Visions of the amputated leg ambush me. Andersson has told me that Mr. Luskin, like many of his amputation patients, elected to have the leg frozen and stored, eventually to be buried with the rest of him. Andersson has also told me that, certain he is doing all he can for his patients, he sleeps soundly. I think about that remarkable self-assurance for the better part of the night.

———————

The next morning, Danny Andersson, refreshed and natty, takes coffee—but no breakfast—early and standing up. Half an hour after rising, he's sitting in his quiet office, in a low brick medical building across a parking lot from the hospital. He's got an hour to work before the help arrives. He sits at his desk amidst a tide of medical journals, leaning stacks of correspondence to sign, medical records, due insurance forms, plaques from the cub scouts and the army, photos of the wife and kids, etchings of the circulatory system from ancient sources, antique clocks ticking and chiming out of sync, and photographs he has taken himself of artfully illuminated pacemakers.

"You reach my stage of a career—established, good referrals, patients calling in the middle of the night whom I've seen before, older patients coming back for second or third operations—and you reach a plateau," Andersson says, talking and signing typed letters at the same time. Today it's notes of thanks and reports of findings to other doctors who have sent patients along. "As medicine increases fees, my income will go up. But I can't get any busier. The next step may be, in fact, to take a partner, to get less busy myself. I don't want to be one of those old surgeons who need to be told when to slow down. I'd like to vacation more, not come in so much in the middle of the night, and I plan to retire early. Surgeons fool themselves if they think they can keep going forever."

He shuffles down through papers and comes up with a red logbook that includes the previous full year of work, "a fairly representative year," he says, from which his mature practice has not often varied. He thumbs through the book and finds a list he's penned in at the end, an extrapolation of operations performed and compensated for in the year's time. It looks like this:

106 arteriograms
141 arterial cases: aortas, femoral-popliteal bypasses, embolectomies, Linton flaps, and redo's
 20 venous cases: veins, portocaval shunts
 65 misc. cases: thoracotomies, skin grafts, amps
 39 Swan-Ganz catheterizations
 97 pacemakers: temporary and permanent

In return for his long hours "as a mother hen," Andersson earns (from the corporation he has set up to receive his billings, pay his rent, the secretaries, and Doreen, and to hold a growing pension fund for all concerned) a salary he has suggested describing as "about the same as that of the chief executive officer of a large U.S. corporation."

He earns a lot of money from his practice, and still more, obviously, from his investment of past earnings. He could live splendidly on a quarter of his pay. He does not feel particularly truculent in discussions about whether this is right.

"My specialty—vascular surgery—is simply an extremely well-paid one. Also, I have become unusually busy. I give up other things. The average surgeon is said to do something like three point five hernia equivalents a week—less than three or four hours of surgery. Each day I do at least one, and frequently two, major procedures—a major arterial reconstruction such as the aorta you saw, a pacemaker installation or replacement, angiograms, bypasses, grafts. I go where I'm needed. I work at three hospitals. They say it takes a population of about 150,000 persons to support someone in my specialty. I don't determine what I get paid."

Blue Shield, the insurance carried by most of Andersson's patients, allows about $2,100 each for aortic replacements, $1,750 for a carotid endarterectomy—cleaning out the plaque in the major arteries of the neck, leading to the brain, an operation usually done twice a week apart, on both sides of the neck. They allow about $1,000 for a pacemaker installation and up to $800 for a typical angiogram.

Andersson obviously enjoys the fact of his good fortune—he lives well, uses leisure heartily, and spares no expense for his family. But he is hazy on the details of its origins. He has to look up the Blue Shield fees for me, although they serve as guide to other third-party payers—insurance companies and Medicare—and form the basis of his income. He also has to look up how much patients are billed for consultation—$40 for a first visit and $20 for subsequent office visits. "It's done in the front office, and the fee schedule changes," he says. He is actively interested in the fate of his wealth, about how to deploy his own capital and the capital that stays in the company he has set up. This company doles out salary, pension plan, and benefits to minimize his tax burden.

"In that sense, it's like any other business," he says. He leaves most investment decisions up to a friend who is a broker in Boston. He consults with the broker often by telephone, and because he is nearly always with patients, they frequently hear one cryptic side of these largely numerical phone conversations-while lying about in paper examining gowns. He favors growth stocks representing new medical technology. He once recommended to me a national company that runs psychiatric and obesity care centers. "Tax shelter oils also make sense, when you have a large income to protect," he has told me. Inside a plexiglass paperweight he keeps on the corner of the office desk are samples of crude oil of various grades.

In spite of his involvement in the stock market, it does not seem that he makes his money because he exercises an especially canny business sense. He is a passionate medical practitioner—the kind who signs guestbooks with an M.D. after his name, and is willing to discuss acquaintances' illnesses with them at cocktail parties. He makes a lot of money because surgical specialists who work hard in fortunate locations do. The fact has to do with the history of medical and surgical lobbies, with the structure of insurance programs and the rights states help reserve for those they license as M.D.s. The political circumstances that have caused surgery to pay well overshadow his private ambition.

The size of his paycheck does affront my basic sense of how much good works ought to bring in. His fees are not the result of dickering in a free market, nor of planning by any kindly social agency. In fact, Andersson says, he would work for half the amount he gets paid, were that the going rate, although he feels he's worth "at least what the next guy gets paid for doing the same thing." And although he's not in it for the money, it would be downright un-American of him not to seize opportunity and advance his family's fortune. It would also be downright saintly of him not to feel some gratitude for all the work the AMA, the

American College of Surgeons, and lobbyists for the insurance companies have done to make this good fortune possible. And he is anything but un-American.

He is so enclosed by his busy practice and so pleased with current arrangements that he has not found time or reason to develop a critical sense of the structure of medicine in America, much less of the economic plights of persons who are not doctors. Reflecting on his fortunate circumstances, he says, "We have something no other country has—you can make any living you want here."

His waiting room has filled with patients, mostly retired factory workers. Doreen and the secretary and the receptionist have come in, and another hard working day in the business of medicine begins.

2

"I Don't Cut Anyone"

Ten thousand surgeons, all heartily engaged in one way or another in the business of medicine, and all fellows or initiates or candidates for membership in the American College of Surgeons, gather annually for the group's Clinical Congress. I join the crowds off loading from planes at the Atlanta airport in an autumn of child murder, and watch about 10 percent of America's working surgeons lining up and signing in at the alphabetized registration booths of the vast Georgia World Congress Center. They crowd onto every floor of the glittering Peachtree, the Omni, the Hyatt Regency, the Atlanta Hilton, and fill a dozen other downtown hotels. They pack into the glass-sided elevators that scale the walls of the Hyatt's towering atrium. And for a week, they run up large tabs at the best restaurants in town.

Americans now spend about three hundred billion dollars a year—nearly 10 percent of the gross national product in 1982—on health care. Some goes for buildings, equipment, and salaries of the many specialized health workers who are not physicians. About 20 percent of it—about fifty billion—goes for doctors' wages, and the majority of that must go to the three-fourths of physicians who are not surgeons. But surgeons, and perhaps especially the active ones who have chosen to come to Atlanta, play especially large roles in the dispersion of the money we spend on medicine. Each surgeon puts hundreds of patients in hospitals every year for the most expensive sorts of care. Many surgeons generate tens—and some, hundreds—of millions of dollars a year each in consequential medical costs. And their own incomes, from medical practice alone averaged about $118,000 in 1982, and some earned double or triple that.

A Hearst science reporter tells me to start work in Atlanta by looking at the wives. She's just come from a pediatricians' conference and she comments that surgeons' wives are inches taller, pounds lighter, and dress more stylishly. "Pediatricians wear bow ties and their wives look frumpy—they also talk to their husbands a lot more than surgeons' wives do." The organizing committee of the College of Surgeons has taken care in assembling for the "spouses" (many wives but few husbands sign up) a welcoming tea and an elaborate social program. They offer an Atlanta House Tour ("We're off . . . for a tour of some of Atlanta's most stately private homes," says the brochure), a Madison, Georgia, House Tour ("You will lunch in an interesting restaurant"), a Victorian House Tour ("Enjoy a never-to-be-forgotten visit to view some of Atlanta's most spectacular . . ."), a Shopping Shuttle ("Atlanta is a shopper's delight!"). The social committee also offers lectures: "Art Collecting for Investment and Pleasure," "Communication and Finance: A Double Whammy for Professional Families," and "Aesthetic Surgery: An Update—aesthetic surgery for the face, neck, eyelids, nose, breast, and abdomen."

Each morning this week, while the wives board buses to tour homes and gather to hear how their husbands' colleagues can take years off thickening necks and drooping eyelids, their husbands traffic in the worldly news of surgery. In the conference center's basement hall a midway of exhibitors' booths has sprung up. Some small companies have rented space to market specialized and newly invented implements; but most of the exhibits represent branches of very large corporations, and they have trucked in and set up posh, eye-catching booths featuring video displays, red carpets, complimentary Cokes, and give-away plastic bags to hold all the literature, printed on heavy stock. One booth features an array of skulls. "How do you do, Doctor . . ." start a hundred thousand smily sales talks before the week is over; surgeons require more costly gear than that used in any other branch of medicine. Surgeons reoutfit their hospitals' surgical suites here. A lot of business gets done.

Standing for a moment near a booth vending operating tables and lamps, I watch one chief of surgery handle the merchandise for a few minutes, then order ten thousand dollars' worth of new shadowless lighting. Drawn by the odor of frying beef, I await my turn in a line of surgeons testing electric scalpels on a row of raw steaks the exhibitor has laid out. BioDynamics-Medical Imaging Division ("Just have a peek into this eyepiece, Doctor?") peddles fiber-optic tubes. Peering into one, I "visualize" the interior of a lifelike plastic spastic colon. Ghastly. I want one. I want to look into my refrigerator through it while the door stays closed, to see if the light really goes off. The Jobst Institute, Inc., sells tight stockings by prescription for persons with vascular problems. Procter & Gamble sells much that a surgeon might want, through their Surgical Products Division. And Whittaker International Services Company (corporate descendant of a publicity group that has long organized public opinion for the AMA) recruits non-Jewish surgeons wishing to spend a year or two operating on Saudi Arabians. Cavitron Lasersonics offers a sleekly housed CO_2 surgical laser, "for precise, non-traumatic, hemostatic removal of tissue."

The biggest booths house two competing surgical staple companies, whose products, recently perfected, represent to their parent companies hopes for big growth. Both sell skin staplers cheaply. "The real profit for the company is in the orders for staples once we get our product into a given hospital," a saleswoman confides. She urges me to squeeze off a few shots into a foam mat. She describes the machine's "several unique features." In front of one company's booth, a robot resembling R2D2 wheels about, worked from a few yards away by a comic with a small microphone pinned to his lapel and a control box palmed in his hand. "Hey, big fellow, don't trip on me," says

27

R2D2 to a very tall surgeon passing by. The surgeon smiles, but keeps moving. A model ("I'm a professional model—they hire girls locally," she says) lies on the display counter of a company selling orthopedic hardware, her healthy arms and legs splendidly splinted with fancy plastic equipment. Marilyn Monroe and Raquel Welch look-alikes provide surgeons with photo opportunities, while pushing Acme United Corporation's "special procedures instrument kits created for one-time use . . . you'll hate to part with them. And that's why they're known as 'The Heartbreakers.'" Roche is here, selling Valium.

A floor above, lectures and films on surgical techniques go on ten at a time, from breakfast session through evening session. In private conference somewhere far above the exhibit hall, a few dozen surgeons, wearing not only the usual name tags but red and purple ribbons indicating official rank in the College of Surgeons, convene to refine the group's policies. Distinguished practitioners in similar halls offer colleagues crash courses— good for required continuing medical education credits back home: no exams, no grades, all on the honor system. The courses have names like "Pancreas I" and "Pancreas II," "Chest Wall Problems," "Reconstruction of the Nose," and "What Has the Endoscopist Actually Added to the Control of Gastrointestinal Cancer?"

And on floors still higher up, cordial corporations, along with alumni associations and regional surgical societies, ply guests with drink and food in hospitality suites each evening. The cardinal rule of the entertainment here is: Never appear chintzy. The hors d'oeuvres are lavish, gaudy, and plentiful— deep-fried lobster chunks, candied chicken legs, shrimp wrapped in bacon, olives the size of plums. Decent champagne. The men in bankers' suits hosting get-togethers here have intense muttered chats with selected guests. Deals must be afoot.

The biggest blast of the season, one that has the surgeons talking the day after, is thrown late in the week by Pacesetter, a company ranking third or fourth in pacemaker sales and wishing to promote its new atrial-ventricular model, which has six programmable features and can be interrogated electronically after installation by surgeons with the right equipment. The company has papered the conference with invitations to a "cabaret evening" in the penthouse of the Peachtree. It features mounds of boiled shrimp, an open bar, and "Night Club Singer Joey English," who is pretty good, and proves upon later investigation to be the wife of the company's vice-president. Dressed in a glittery costume and accompanied by a band, she pours gutsy sexuality into unlikely lyrics. "Did you know my heart beats for your love?" she croons to each shrimp-chomping surgeon there, as lights dim and muted trumpets follow her into a quiet mood. Then to the blare of "Hey, Big Spender," hips writhing, she belts out the company come-on:

> Hey, Pacesetter—
> The minute you walked in the room
> I could see you were a man of distinction,
> A real Pacesetter,
> Good-looking, ah, so refined . . .
> Don't you know you really are ahead of your time?
> Hey, Pacesetter—
> Wouldn't you like to have
> Six, six, six [did she say six?]
> Parameters?
> It's multifunctional Programalith—
> Let's get right to the point—
> I don't interrogate
> For anyone but you.
> Hey, Pacesetter—pace a little while with me.

This evening, I'm in no-man's-land with all the other big spenders, and the unchintziness makes sense. It's a fine thing to be important.

Andersson, who usually attends these annual events, has not flown south for this one. "People got mugged right outside the door at the last one," he had said. In search of a Virgil to guide me in his stead, I haunt the New England Medical Society's reception, where I know a few people, and I eventually fall in with the right surgeon. His name is Russell Stearne. We talk for a while and he volunteers himself, then gets right down to business. He doesn't waste time.

We wander through the technical exhibits—he stops to shoot a few skin staples. We settle down for coffee at a balcony café and look down into the crowded lobby of the Congress Center. For a week solid, twenty hours a day, I realize, there's seldom been a single step on the wide escalators below us that has not carried two surgeons rising and then two surgeons descending. For a moment I suffer the delusion that we have stopped for our coffee right by the heavenly gates. I imagine that the surgeons stepping off at the top, two by two, are there making deals with the good Lord on behalf of their patients, then descending again, to buy the right stuff, to learn whatever it takes to be most helpful to the afflicted, to do right by their shared profession.

Stearne is a dark man, with striking, deep-set brown eyes that flick past me from face to face as we seat ourselves. He is of middling height, is in his late forties, weighs twenty pounds more, he confesses as he eyes a display of cakes, than he did when he went to Harvard. He still has a full crown of black hair, and it seems to have been cut by a barber trained in the early fifties, when sideburns were grounds for suspecting the wearer of Communist sympathies. He's beyond suspicion. Within moments, he's told me that he's a staunch Reagan man, that nothing's more important to him than his family, that most surgeons are ill-educated outside their fields, that he majored in English at Harvard, and that he loves his work. What else do I want to know? I'm interested in surgeons. For starters, I say, in whether there's some toll, some isolation and separateness that he might experience because of the specialness of a trade that has him cutting sleeping people open all day.

"Cut?" Stearne asks, with what I take to be a tone of mock surprise and a look of mock innocence. "I don't cut anyone."

I say that when any man slips a knife under the skin of someone fast asleep, and tugs it forward, severing flesh, drawing blood, he's surely, and at the very least, cutting someone, no matter what the context and what his profession and intention.

30

"But no!" Stearne protests. "I never cut anyone." He still keeps a straight, downright cherubic, expression on his round face. Having just met him, I have no idea how to take his semantic perversity—whether to think that he's stubborn but dull, and doesn't know quite what he's saying, or that he's got a number he runs by lay persons he encounters and has now embarked upon it. "I don't cut anyone," he declares. "That's not what I do."

"Look at this coin," he says, taking two empty hands and raising them away from the doughnuts on the table—we've settled for doughnuts, not cake. He rotates his left hand over his right at a distance of a few inches. A coin appears, not gripped between thumb and forefinger, the way civilians with opposable thumbs hold small things on display, but lodged in the crease between third and fourth fingers, canted above the back of his hand like a vandalized gravestone—the way magicians hold coins.

He waves his free hand again, and the coin turns into a draped scarf.

"Heads or tails?" he asks with delight. A smile touches the innocence of his face. "You see? I don't cut my patients." He shakes his head to emphasize the denial. "Things are not always what they appear to be. I never cut my patients. I operate. I *fix* people."

We drink our coffee in silence while I get the point. The man is entertaining. "New guide likes razzle-dazzle," I write in my notebook.

"You've seen some surgery?"

"Some," I say.

"But you probably haven't seen any heroic surgery."

I probably haven't.

Stearne says, "The ideal patient for me to operate on would be the one who is well. All they have to worry about is me. The next best is the younger patient with only one thing wrong, and the rest of the body working well—you fix the one thing and home they go. But real-life practice isn't like that. We operate on old people, and they usually have many things wrong with them. It's been said that you can justify at least three surgical procedures on anyone in America over the age of sixty-five. Heroic surgery is a different matter altogether. Here you don't expect to win. I don't often have to do it—an emergency once in a while. It always bothers me to lose someone."

———

They're showing films. The "festival"—that's what they call it—movies all week long, in an auditorium that seems as big as Radio City, film after film, frequently narrated in person by the surgeon filmed, of procedures rare and innovative, or standard and impeccably executed. Tonight's films will attract the largest crowd; they deal with those lengthy and technically difficult procedures even the proudest general surgeon would routinely pass along to specialists at the biggest teaching hospitals. The event will be the equivalent of a hiking club meeting to watch films of daring Alpine ascents.

A surgeon I encounter explains what's going on. Surgeons call what they do "heroic surgery" when they undertake procedures with higher than usual failure rates. They usually attempt such operations only when the patient is a sure goner unless something's done. Surgeons normally achieve mortality rates of well under 1 percent for common procedures such as appendectomies—almost no one dies from such surgery. More ticklish procedures, such as major vascular replacements on very sick patients, may have mortality rates nearer 4 or 5 percent. To some extent, surgeons can control their mortality rates by operating on stronger patients. In the operations to be shown tonight, mortality rates of 40 or 50 percent are common. Heroic surgery is done on poor candidates.

Stearne, and his colleagues entering the auditorium, can endure the daily mayhem of their profession, one suspects, because they enter each job armored and cherish their protection. As they gather, they laugh jovially, pound the backs of long-lost colleagues, light each other's cigars, and wait for the show of heroic works to begin. What surgeons "seem to do with their strong feelings about emotionally upsetting aspects of their work," medical sociologist Renée Fox has written, "is to push them just below the surface of their consciousness. That these feelings are not deeply buried is suggested by how easily they can be aroused." The surgeons in the theater are boisterous as they wait for the lights to dim.

In other fields, heroes don't gain kudos by doing what heroic surgeons do. Policemen who get medals pinned to their swelling chests by mayors, at special ceremonies with their buddies watching at attention, earn their credit by crawling out on thin ice to rescue six-year-olds. Firemen earn citations for heroism as they rush back into burning buildings moments before walls collapse, load up with coughing baby triplets, and stagger back outside, hats on fire. Heroic soldiers run at Jerry bunkers, machine guns ablaze, giving their pinned-down buddies time to retreat. What the policemen, firemen, and soldiers do, in life-and-death situations, that surgeons seem not to do, is place themselves in physical danger, volunteer to die on behalf of others.

As long as Stearne does what colleagues think is "the right thing" (and this heroic surgery film festival helps stretch the limits of "the right thing"), he will face no danger, even if he loses a patient. No Hammurabi will vivisect him in turn. The county medical society won't kick him out; the hospital's mortality committee won't even suspend his privileges. Following heroic but fatal procedures, he may spend the rest of the day going on with the other chores of a life built of brief but intense efforts to battle death, heaped upon each other.

He will have faced a certain menace nonetheless—not from thin ice, bullets, or smoke, but from his proximity to death. The danger is to one's easiness, not one's body. Death nearby scares everyone, even these pros.

But now row upon row of adjacent surgeons study the program complacently. The hall darkens. A doctor from Hong Kong, named Wong, begins to narrate from the lectern a film called "Pharyngo-Laryngo-Esophagectomy with Pharyngo-Gastric Anastomosis." For this show the volume is turned nearly all the way down—but for some reason we can still hear the film's recorded sound track dimly. It's as if Dr. Wong has embarked upon a simultaneous translation from a private language of his own that no one else understands. The film plays. The splitting of the chest and the opening of the belly proceed, Wong says, "routinely." I have little sense I'm watching the cutting of a human being. Dr. Wong speaks exclusively in the passive voice—"A further incision was made"—giving the impression that neither he nor, for that matter, anyone at all has done what is happening on the screen. A purple tube leading to the neck comes into view as the tissue above it is retracted. Wong's flashlight, which projects a little white arrow of brightness, darts like a dragonfly along the length of the purple tube, while Wong's voice, thinned to reedy telephonic fidelity by the sound system, says, ". . . next, the esophagus is displayed."

The film demonstrates a technique, a doctor whispers to me, not commonly practiced in America, for dealing with advanced esophageal cancer. Wong points his light at his own disembodied hands on the screen. The hands, armed with scalpel, are displaying in turn the esophagus, the throat, the stomach. The flashlight arrow dabs at the swollen signs of advanced disease. It points to Wong's hands removing many parts of the body. The diseased esophagus goes. The film skips time. The hands, gloved and quick, rehang the stomach higher up, and stitch it in just under the throat. This is a palliative operation, when it works. Nearly a third of the patients he's tried it on have died on the table, he says. Those on whom this surgery "succeeds" live more months than they would have otherwise— but they still seem to have cancer. I feel like a hero just watching.

After this film, I take in "Transcervical Thymectomy for Myasthenia Gravis" and "Interposition Mesocaval Shunt for Portal Hypertension." We leave amidst the flow of surgeons, who gesticulate and shout, now even more excited than they were on entering, by what they've seen, by its virtuosity. The evening's films suggest impressively the great range of surgeons' redemptive powers.

In the aisle I run into Stearne again. His mind wanders associatively. "In Russia, I hear, they now have developed a disinfectant so powerful, yet nonastringent, that surgeons can use it on their hands, and then operate without gloves on."

We move toward the doors. I ask, "Would you like to try it? Could it be of help while you work—give you a more sensitive touch?"

"I wouldn't ever care to use that disinfectant," he says. "It might be handy once in a while to feel things a little better. What bothers me would be touching the patient. I like gloves. I don't want to *touch* that *stuff*—that disease."

———————

Weeks later, Russell Stearne, gloveless and seated at table, dark eyes aglow, is touching food—some indeterminate sandwich on a grinder roll, perhaps the barbecue. His chin darts momentarily over his plate. He's back from Atlanta, returned to the usual life of active surgeons, which centers in the nation's seven thousand hospitals. Surgeons need workshops. The spreading use of anesthesia after the middle of the last century, and the introduction of aseptic operating techniques almost fifty years after that, expanded the mandate to cut. Surgical mortality from shock and infection fell quickly. Hospitals transformed themselves from storage places for the dying poor to places where cure might be attempted—places with cafeterias. In the morning just gone by, Stearne has completed (in one and a half hours' time) two hernias and an appendectomy, operating, as he does most mornings, before seeing his hospitalized patients. After lunch, as he does four days a week, he will see patients in his office.

Grinder in hand, he is trying to swear off food. I have noticed, as we changed out of surgical greens, that a vest of extra flesh girds his blocky form. He regrets it, and has finally been moved toward resolve, if not action, by the prospect of competition. "My twenty-fifth Harvard reunion's coming up," he says, "and I want to look more like I did when I was an undergraduate than anyone else there does." He bites into the sandwich. One day it may be the barbecue—which Stearne claims later never to have tried—and the next, fish squares saturated with cooking oil, then slathered with house salad spread. Grapeade drink, optional croutons, foam rubber angel food cake.

Stearne prefers operating on a full stomach, "although if I'm too busy to eat, it doesn't bother me a bit." And he likes his mealtime banter. Elsewhere in the hospital, hierarchy shows in every casual josh, but in this age of humanized physicians and unionized nurses, dining time is somewhat exempt from usual protocol. Several nurses, and even one young orderly, join Stearne for the meal. Outside of work, Stearne is a listener and a questioner, not a tale teller. His questions are awkwardly direct, and his quips put him in the best light. He seems to have at his command a perpetually updated index of the familial situations and hopes of dozens of hospital staff members and hundreds of patients. As lunch progresses, he names absent spouses, mentions colleges and military bases where children have gone to live, quotes from previous chats, some of which took place months before.

Most days, his lunches follow this pattern. He likes the hospital world and stays there for more hours each morning than seem necessary to accomplish his work. Weeks later, a few days after the Harvard reunion, over lunch again, I ask him about the event.

"I remembered everyone's name I ever knew while there."

But had he succeeded in his private competition to look more as he had as an undergraduate than anyone else?

"No one had any trouble recognizing me, either."

⸺◆⸺

After lunch we leave the hospital and bicycle, through crisp weather and falling leaves, the several blocks back to his office. He strides across the crowded waiting room without looking up, heading for the safety of the offices that lie beyond the receptionist's desk, his gray tweed sports jacket flapping around him. This is the way most people first see their doctors. No one present has trouble recognizing him. Many patients seek eye contact, but the surgeon has gone shy, like a waitress who won't even glance at her charges for fear of being sent off for a glass of ice water. His office is barer and larger than Danny Andersson's. A copy of Rembrandt's *Anatomy Lesson* hangs across from a modern desk.

Stearne's practice differs from Andersson's. Stearne is a general surgeon, and for the most part, he tells me, he competes head-to-head with the most active half-dozen other local general surgeons, and less directly, with surgeons in the several major cities within a morning's drive of his town. Stearne keeps no annual log. But he estimates that he does some three hundred procedures each year, most frequently the common ones—hernias, appendixes, gall bladders. His work is eclectic. He sees "some of everything." He does a fair amount of cancer work, performs many of the same types of vascular operations that Andersson does, and handles the nonorthopedic aspects of traumatic emergencies. He had a year's training in London with a famous hepatic surgeon, and occasionally has the opportunity to practice this rather uncommon specialty on patients "with operable liver disease."

In addition to his private, fee-for-service work, Stearne does an atypical amount of "prepaid" surgery—it's called that within the profession, as if "prepaid" refers to a body part upon which a surgeon works rather than to the payment plan his patients use. Stearne has three partners, including another general surgeon his own age, Theodore Culver, and two semiretired senior surgeons. In the 1930s, the older men were the first around to be board certified by the American College of Surgeons, and because of that were throughout their careers regarded by many in their city as "the classy practice," as one oldtimer put it.

The most senior of these men, a stately Yankee now in his eighties and very active in the physicians' antinuclear movement, recalls first considering Russell Stearne for the partner-

37

ship fifteen years back. "Dr. Culver was with us already, and I was reaching the time—about sixty-five—when I'd planned to do other things I found interesting while I still could. Dr. Stearne was looking into this area. He was very well trained both in New York and England. That attracted us, and we liked him. Also he was board certified. We never even took him in the operating room and watched him operate first. I suppose that was something we might have done, but we didn't."

During the office's long history, it has accumulated a variety of contracts for its partners to do emergency work and hold clinics at local factories. And about ten years back, when a health management organization—an HMO—grew up alongside the local university's health service, the partnership signed on to supply their consulting and operating services—for a fee per-head-enrolled. Currently the HMO and the student health service together guarantee the surgical practice payments totaling about $100,000 a year. Stearne and Culver spend an afternoon a week each visiting patients at the HMO and they do what surgery is required.

The connection, which, along with their factory contract work, assures the partnership a minimum annual income, has cost it other business. The staunchest of the old guard of local family doctors, inculcated with the AMA's early abhorrence of group practice (a stance it has altered) and of prepaid medical service, have barely spoken to Stearne since his partnership signed on with the HMO. And none of the patients waiting for Stearne out in the reception area has been referred to the partnership by these older doctors.

"The HMO work is a big part of my case load," Stearne says. "It's a young population because it has many college students, but you'd be surprised what we do. Lots of appendixes, of course. But also breast biopsies, cancer, gall bladders, some vascular surgery, ulcers, hernias—especially the farm boys. It's good surgery—those youngsters with only one thing wrong with them."

I tell Stearne about some recent studies comparing the frequency of operations under prepaid and fee-for-service schemes. Prepaid surgeons appear to be almost three times as busy; they do an average of about ten "hernia equivalents" a week. On salary or contract, they earn far less per operation than surgeons paid by the piece. The prepaid surgeons do a greater proportion of "ambulatory" surgery, sending more patients home to mend thriftily, out of the hospital. Another study shows that prepaid surgeons (who earn the same amount whether or not they operate) are far more conservative about operating at all—they do so far less frequently per unit of population. Still another study observed two forms of prepaid surgical services, treating similar populations: one group that reimbursed its surgeons by the operation and the other that paid a fixed yearly rate. Appendectomies were 140 percent more frequent when paid for by the procedure. Tonsillectomies were 450 percent higher. And hysterectomies were 630 percent higher. Stearne is interested in the numbers. He is in the unusual position of doing both sorts of work. He says his decisions are based on symptoms, not payment plans. "I may not be the best-paid surgeon in town," he says, "but I am one of the busiest. And when the HMO expands—which it's doing now—we're in an excellent position to do well." His HMO connection seems to have developed from the seizing of a business opportunity and not from any ideological preference that led him away from fee-for-service medicine.

In fact, Stearne's corporation once had another minor source of income—and although it was a fee-for-service one, it was nevertheless also at odds with the beliefs of the town's old-guard doctors. In a large and gaudy shopping mall, an enterprising, thick-skinned young internist had started a "walk-in" medical center. He competed with every shopper's family doctor. He competed with the hospital emergency room. No appointments necessary. Easy access. Short waits. And, pagan among the pious, the internist advertised intensively on local television. The ads had gone so far as to show this man of science at work, reading X-rays, even examining patients. They also announced that "vasectomies are performed." Stearne was briefly the surgeon who came in and performed them. He spent Saturday

39

mornings at it, taking about twenty minutes with each walk-in patient, and collecting about ten dollars a minute. "I thought the vasectomy patients would be backpacker types," Stearne says, "but that's not who came. It was middle-aged men, and they told me they'd wanted to do this for a while, but before they saw the TV ads they just hadn't had a place they knew it was done."

Stearne's varied sorts of work keep him traveling about several towns, from clinic to office to hospital. He writes off the cost of a Mercedes every three years as business expense. Together, his various surgical enterprises earn him a substantial income—about half as much as Andersson makes doing only fee-for-service medicine from his office a few counties away.

3

"You've Got to
Insulate Yourself"

I peer out through the receptionist's window at Stearne's waiting room. A pile-up of patients has gathered there now—he's running late. They sit in wooden spindle chairs, leaning back against the Harvard insignia and motto: "Veritas." Some read year-old *Time* magazines. The afternoon holds much in store, Stearne tells me. A few of the patients out there have been referred by general practitioners who suspect their patients may have cancer. Two will be told they do: one has already learned on his last visit that he might; the second is about to hear her first news on the subject. Patients will present the minor problems of used bodies—hangnail, hernia, hemorrhoids. Several will discuss their postoperative woes following small repairs Stearne has made upon them—stitches will come out of a cut leg, the surgeon will peek at a patched nostril, torn in a car crash and rather handsomely sewn, and he will also reconsider the infected closure of a diabetic's mashed toe. He will examine a woman who has had colon surgery, a baby who had a hernia, and a girl who needed skin grafts. A patient will consult Stearne about vascular problems. Carotid bruits will whisper like fatal rifle ricochets sounding through his stethoscope earpieces. And one patient will complain that her belly always hurts some, but not much, lately, and that the family doctor can't find anything wrong.

The patients must feel ambivalent about the black-haired doctor who ambles, eyes still averted, back within view of the waiting room (far behind schedule now, with a white lab coat slipped on instead of the sports jacket). Some may anticipate relief from their anxieties about whatever ails them. But the prospect of relief is built upon the dread—well-founded in the case of the round-faced, blank-eyed young woman in a white dress, reading in the far corner—that things may be worse than one dared imagine.

"I suppose I like some of the surgery better than some of the difficult office encounters," Stearne says. This cheerful, wary, and self-protective man represents hope, desperate hope, to some of the patients assembled. And were he ever to permit himself to feel their emotions full-blast, he might turn and bolt for the exit, the white coat flapping in the wind, while his patients, already cross from long waiting, scowl after the fleeing figure.

He stays. He doesn't even seem to think of leaving. He does say, "I wish I had a back door."

Then, chatting about the very good bicycle included in the tag sale he's staging because his family is moving across town, he pulls out the first patient's folder and sets to his work.

He nods to the attendant receptionist. A thin-lipped, seventy-year-old plumber in green work clothes gets the call. He's got a nice, easy smile. The receptionist herds him into the examining room. Stearne has told me about him. His first wife died a few years back, of cancer. Then he'd gone to plumb a country farm for a retired lawyer and his wife—"from Minnesota, Quaker couple," Stearne had said—and had ended up married to the lawyer's wife and living on the farm. He'd developed an ulcer, though. Another surgeon had sewn up the ulcer, and had also sewn the poor plumber's intestine closed. He'd almost starved before Stearne had figured out his trouble and gone in after it.

"Was this an avoidable error? Negligence? Was it actionable? It sounds that way to me."

"It just happens. It's not the kind of thing that's actionable. But with every patient who comes in here, there's cause for concern. Every doctor gets suits these days."

We walk in to see the plumber. He's in good shape, blue-eyed and wiry, lean as a jockey, mild as a vicar. Stearne prods his abdomen for a while, then slaps his butt. The plumber leaves, smiling. Stamped cured.

In the adjacent examining room, a tiny patient glances away as Stearne enters, somber-faced. The patient continues feeding from his mother's breast. The patient's aunt watches through rheumy eyes, while the mother flashes an earthy, gap-toothed grin. She's an Ecuadorian Indian. Yet here she is in the office. She looks sturdy, with hearty unselfconscious expressions. By her forthright tending of the child, she's redefining Stearne's quarters as outlandish, high-toned. She presents the baby. He's fat, drooling, football-headed, smiling, olive-skinned, swaddled in baby pink. Stearne peels away the wrappings and feels a tiny incision on its abdomen, reddened but healing. He had a strangulated hernia. There's no mortality threatening here. The baby laughs. Stearne laughs. The baby's aunt laughs. The baby's mother says, "Sí." Another butt slapped. Another cure.

Back in the first examining room, the patient is noticeably beautiful, with thin blond hair and delicate spare-lined features. Her right cheek is purple with bruises. She wears an examining gown. Her husband, large, drab, in brown slacks and a blue work shirt, stands awkwardly across the room. She, too, is holding a baby. She hands it to her husband and moves painfully onto the examining table. They were in a car accident a week ago. She states complaints. Stearne touches, concludes, and addresses the husband: "If there's a bruise between the ovary and the uterus, it will go down and it won't interfere with her reproductive function." Stearne says to her, gesturing, "You'll have twelve more like that one." The glowing, friendly baby faces the action, amused by whatever he makes of the doctor from his father's arms.

In the hallway between patients, Stearne says, "You're going to think this next old man is a religious fanatic." The old man, tight-skinned and sharp-chinned, strides forward and shakes Stearne's hand, as if about to sell him a car. While still offering exuberant greetings, the man bends down and pulls both woolen pants cuffs up above his knees. "You praying too much again?" Stearne shouts into the man's deaf ear. The man lets out a belly laugh. "Tell us again how you got those," shouts Stearne. Discolored, purplish patches of skin, ringed with large stitches, cover both knees, purple patches on pink pants.

"I'm retired," says the man, "and I was doing some masonry work—floating a poured floor for my son-in-law. I guess I don't have much feeling left in my legs anymore. When I got up, my knees were like looking down into hamburger. The doctor here did some skin grafts."

"He didn't get it in church, after all," says Stearne, and we laugh.

A fair woman in her late forties, with a crown of graying hair, tries to read Stearne's blank face as he enters the other examining room. She's had a mammogram; it's shown a slight shadow on the X-ray. "I don't think it's a meaningful finding, and neither does the radiologist at the hospital. If this were anything to worry about, there ought to be a palpable mass where the X-ray suggests one. And there isn't. If there were, I could feel it. Don't worry. Come back in six months for a re-exam. Come to me." The woman smiles, and sweetly nods assent, speechless.

Out in the corridor, Stearne says, "These office hours aren't always as grim as you might think. It's very rewarding to see some patients." On to the next.

I find it difficult to imagine Stearne's experience. His sureness of his skill, and his detachment from the prospects of these patients, are exotic, beyond any experience that can be shared by those of us with more usual burdens. Do his professionalized feelings flatten the mystery of life? Is he merely an equable witness to actuarial artifact—observing in flesh and blood the statistics of particular diseases as they work out relentlessly, as per schedule, with due exemption and due risk, ho hum?

I've glimpsed terror in the hearts of just two surgeons. One, by far the most literate of the rare breed of surgeon writers, Richard Selzer, admits to it in cold type in books such as *Mortal Lessons,* and by doing so has earned a literary following, and also the scorn of many of his surgeon readers (who ask what I think of him, and then ward off my praise). The other, a rural surgeon and philosopher, feels impelled to take a year off now and then, during which he consorts with social scientists and government officials on problems of ethics. Most surgeons keep their fearfulness hidden, even from themselves.

Stearne welcomes Mrs. Smith, who leaves laughing, and, many patients later, the young Mrs. Jones, who leaves crying. Stearne's ability to offer reassurances, patient after patient, one dilemma after another, good verdict and dreadful news alike, demonstrates the miracle of insularity that keeps him going year after year. He awaits a final patient, who has phoned saying she's on her way.

Between patients, in his office, he is like an actor between scenes. The costume remains; the character alters. On stage, he's measured and gentle, a mere representative of a larger body of knowledge and skill, doing what can be done. He never relaxes with patients. Even when friends come in to be treated, he is surgeon first. He quotes numbers whenever he explains things— usually odds. With the help of science and technology (he gives patients to understand), he reacts to disease as best he can. The numbers help demonstrate to patients that he's reasonable and deliberate, and give some slim grounds for cheer about something or another, even in the worst of cases.

Off stage, he frolics. His face grows mobile. He laughs, he changes the subject, he utters personal thoughts and evaluations he may not utter in public. The nurses and receptionist occasionally receive his confidences. But it is his partner, Ted Culver, who hears the worst Stearne has to say. The two, who rarely socialize off duty, have shared thousands of operations over the past fifteen years.

Their older partners seem to have been more august, always on stage, perhaps even with themselves. Intergenerational communication in the office stayed formal in the years all four worked together. The new generation reveals itself more readily. Stearne and Culver are rivals, in a brotherly way. Stearne says of Culver, "He won't let go of a patient for love or money, even when he's going out of town." And Culver says that Stearne would never do his paperwork, "if someone like me didn't keep him in line."

With one another, they have managed to supersede the proud autonomy that almost seems to define surgeons. They quip—frequently soothingly—between patients. They confer with knowledge of how each of their personalities influences medical judgment. It's a lucky alliance, which shelters both men and improves the quality of care each offers.

"She's here, Doctor," says the receptionist, standing on one foot, tipped and leaning in past the door to the office. The patient, a janitor in a factory, comes rolling up the hallway with the swagger of a street tough. She's sixty, stocky and untidy, her dyed-red hair spilling from a babushka, one blue blouse tail unstuck from dirty red stretch pants that sweep outward upon a jouncing belly. She looks about repeatedly as she follows Stearne next door, into an examining room. She smells of stale powder and cigarette smoke. He points, and she sits up on the table, chubby legs dangling. He takes a wooden tongue depressor and a flashlight, and looks in her mouth. He reaches a finger in after the tongue depressor and feels what he has seen, touching disease. The doctor, ungloved, touches a patient and what he touches could not be uglier.

Two years before, he had managed to peel a tongue cancer from this same spot, and radiation had further stifled the tumor there. She had been able to forget it, and even Stearne had suspected she might be cured. But now she's having trouble swallowing. It must have been back for some time. She pulls Stearne's hand away.

"Another look, please, Mrs. O'Leary," he says, and replaces his hand.

She pouts with her eyes, and issues small glottal grunts of frustration. There's nothing attractive or glamorous or heroic about this late-afternoon piece of work. She's peevish—she must be afraid. A marble-sized tumor has grown up under the raspy stubble on the back of her tongue. It swells from the padded floor of the mouth like a small boulder in a field, with grass grown right over it. It rises up so high that Stearne's penlight throws an arc of its shadow across the shimmering stalactite of her uvula.

She doesn't want to realize what has happened. As soon as Stearne takes his hand away, she shouts out, "I don' wanna have to not work, like last time. How long will I be out, Doc?"

"We can't tell that yet. Now you wait here for a moment, will you?"

We go down the corridor, to find Culver in his office. Stearne's reaction to surgically treatable conditions is to want to do something. "If you have a minute, Ted, will you see what you think?" Stearne himself thinks the going will be "treacherous, at best." He thinks the woman will not be cured by surgery, although she may once again be saved for a while. But this time, to get at the tumor, he will have to split her jaw and take away the left side of her jawbone, remove the tumor, and finally reconstruct a new jaw in the aftermath. This palliative treatment will take many months and several operations.

Stearne reenters the examining room, and introduces Culver: "This is the doctor who helps me operate." Culver looks. Then the two men leave again.

"You going to operate?" Culver asks in the hallway.

"Do what I can."

"What can you do?" Culver turns Stearne's phrase around. "The lady hasn't got much time, and the operation would be so extensive, she'd barely heal before . . ."

"I think there's more hope than that," says Stearne.

"Another opinion? Who'd you use? Mike Bell down in New Haven?" Culver knows Bell in New Haven never wants to operate on cases like this. Stearne goes into the examining room again. And he does send the lady on for a second opinion—to Sam Pincus in Boston. Pincus is less conservative than Bell. "The other doctor will help me?" she asks as she leaves.

A week later, Sam Pincus's opinion arrives by mail in the office: Operate if you think it will help. I ask Stearne if he's now going ahead with the job, and it becomes clear that, once seconded, he's edged closer to his partner's caution.

"We'll see if chemotherapy can knock it back enough so we can have a better shot at it. I'll do whatever I can to save my patients."

———————

Cutters, bearers of hope and doom, distant but avuncular, surgeons cannot be what they must be to please. They fail time after time, with the lives of our relatives and friends in their hands. Their successes are painful enough to evoke quizzical responses even in those they heal. In the office, their work fosters such feelings of dependency that seriously ill patients may imagine they're talking to someone other than the surgeon altogether, someone especially protective. The dads they had when they were small. The Pope. Or just that generic authoritative figure, Doc. Patients call Stearne "Doc" most often when most helpless. Being a surgeon has got to be as wearing as being beautiful, and even more likely to tempt with prospects of power, because there's more to be had, and for longer.

A classmate Stearne remembers vaguely from Harvard, Arnold Marglin, wrote of his fatigue with the role of doctor in their twenty-fifth-reunion yearbook: "Flattery, arrogance, uncontested authority, then self-deception, ensconcement in our unearned see."

The next day is just the same for Stearne. Surgery. Horrible lunch. Crossing a waiting room full of patients. He is consumed by what he does. He goes home for supper, half the days of the year, with his on-call beeper clipped to his waist. He doesn't seem to mind; in fact, he signs up for additional duty at the hospital emergency room. He finds new patients there, and fee-for-service patients, at that. But he is no hungry fledgling, nor so avaricious he doesn't savor time off. He simply likes the work and how it makes him feel. He tells very ill patients they may call him at home. He has a fine phone manner, and on such calls seems unrushed, informative, and generous with reassurance. When the beeper reaches for him while he is at the dinner table, halfway through the roast or awaiting the soufflé, he goes. His children are used to it; they keep right on talking.

It's a problem most of the surgeons I've met never resolve. From an article, "Effects of Stress on Physicians and Their Medical Practice," by Jack McCue, M.D., in the *New England Journal of Medicine*, February 25, 1982:

> Retreat from family life is probably the most common adaptation to the demands of medical practice. . . . Spontaneous home activities are interrupted by the telephone or pocket pager; late office hours, hospital rounds on days off, and subtle or unconscious encouragements for patients to call after hours erode the time and energy needed for personal development.
>
> . . . The first reason is peer pressure. . . . The second reason is fear of failure. . . . A final factor is self-importance. Insecure physicians can maximize ego gratification at the hospital, where they issue orders, make critical decisions, and receive praise from their patients; at home, the physician is just another suburban husband.

This suburban husband married young. His eldest child, a boy, has headed off to college, and the elder of his two girls is not far behind. His younger boy is still in elementary school. The household retains vestiges of formality. To Sterne's children I am introduced and reintroduced, always as "mister."

"I had more freedom than I allow my kids," he tells me, on a Sunday morning that has progressed from late breakfast nearly to noon free of emergency summons. "From when I was thirteen until sixteen or so—I don't know if it was me or them—I'd grown up setting myself up as independent, as outside a group, showing you didn't need people."

Stearne is a lavish provider. When I visit, I see children forever heading off to lessons. They retreat in summer and on snowy weekends—sometimes with their father along and sometimes with mother alone—to a condominium on a North Country ski slope. And the family has just moved to a very large house, which Stearne dreamed about for years, and finally helped architects to design.

"The architects showed me the preliminary plans," he says, pacing and gesturing beyond the high stark ceilings of a huge glass- and cement-walled living room crossed by an angled cat-walk. The room is larger than two squash courts. "They said, 'Here, it's got a twenty-by-twenty-foot living room.' I said, 'I don't want a twenty-by-twenty living room. I want one thirty-six by thirty-six.' I didn't realize just how big such a room would be." He looks around it, still chagrined, and shakes his head.

Stearne's new dream house spreads across a half-landscaped hilltop, above a hundred acres of fields and woods. V-shaped, like some Noah's ark beached atop a Yankee Ararat, the building looks down from five miles' distance upon the city hospital's red smokestack and the white steeple of the Congregational church. The starboard side of the house contains the big living room, pantries, utility closets, a tiled kitchen leading out to a gravel-floored greenhouse, and above all this, guest rooms and a very ample master bedroom.

The port side of the house Stearne calls "the children's wing." Downstairs, a corridor connects the two sections. Upstairs there's no connection at all. Rooms adjacent but in different wings have solid walls between them. Corridors end. "I designed that into it. From the kids' rooms, they have to go downstairs, then up the other side."

"Why?"

"They like it. I think it will work out this way, too. I like to spend time with my kids. I like kids in general. In fact, I almost became a pediatrician.

"In medical school, you're impressionable. They have good lecturers, and whichever impresses you on that rotation, that's what you want to be then. I wanted to be a psychiatrist for a while, even. I was good at it—got excellent review reports.

"But I admired the chief of pediatrics a lot. It's interesting medicine, in young bodies. Not a million things wrong at once.

I'd even gone to see about a residency. Then came my surgical rotation. It was the middle of the night. They brought in a policeman by ambulance, who had been stabbed with a broken bottle, right in the temporal artery. It was a mess—looked worse than it was. Blood spurted out of his head like the Fountain of Versailles, up to the ceiling. No one put pressure on it—just screamed and rushed him down to the minor surgery room. I was on the team. It was exciting.

"As we rushed down the hall, there, at two in the morning, was a little rumpled pediatrician, talking on the phone. I went by, hand on the stretcher, and I caught a few words he was saying into the phone. A few—but they were enough. They made up my mind.

"'Well, mother,' he said, 'maybe if you boiled the milk a little longer, the baby won't vomit so often.' Lights flashed. Boy, did they ever.

"I realized right then I didn't want to be spending the rest of my life up at two A.M. telling mothers how to cook babies' formula. At that instant, I had decided on surgery."

Stearne, on-call beeper still clipped to his belt, takes a green-webbed lawn chair under his arm and sets up among the hanging plants of the gravel-floored greenhouse, past an arch, just beyond the kitchen. He decides upon a section of the Sunday *New York Times*. Sports first. He reads, snapping the pages, while family life goes on around him. The older kids study. The younger ones play outside. Stearne watches them through the greenhouse windows, as they tumble on the lawn. His wife washes the breakfast dishes. "This is what I dreamed of doing in here," he says. Sun streams in upon the surgeon's smiling face.

———————◆———————

A few days further into fall, across a hundred miles of mountains and timberland, and a world away, Danny Andersson has kissed his own family, driven to the office, and now prepares to take on all comers. The big chrome tape player sits on the floor of his office behind the desk, like a pet dog. Sunlight gleams from the top of his bald head. He sends Doreen to fetch his first patient of the day.

"Vascular surgery is a court of last resort," he says. "I see mostly older patients with serious problems. I give my patients more time. Some cases I can't give more time, but I can improve the quality of the time they have left. How do I do this? I make them more independent. Keep them on their feet, shopping, out of the old-age home. If I can't do that? Maybe in a home I can keep them going to the bathroom and not having to use a bedpan. Or if they have to be in bed, I can give them a below-the-knee amp and not an above-the-knee, so they can still hike themselves up on the bedpan without help. I do as much as I can."

The woman whom Doreen now ushers in seems caught in mid-flinch. Wiry and delicate, on the margin of old age, she has dyed her hair blond and wears tight plaid slacks. She cocks her head to the left and crooks her neck, perhaps out of anxiety. A squinting expression stays on her face as she speaks. She has just noticed that far above her a landslide has begun tumbling.

"I've always been healthy," she says. Her voice is thin. She gestures vigorously, but her voice has a winsome melody. "Yet a few days ago—I don't know *what* happened. Suddenly there were flashing lights, and half my vision seemed to go. It only lasted for a while. The family doctor said to come to you." She's had something like a stroke, Andersson tells her. A "transient ischemic attack"—a TIA—frequently the first signal of advanced vascular disease. Andersson leads her, personally, by the arm and slowly, to the examining table down the hall. He sounds pulses. He prods her belly with his fingers. He is frank. "This is troublesome. I also feel a fairly significant swelling of the aorta here. I want you to have some pictures taken of it— there's a radiologist in this same medical building, just down the hall. We'll get you in there now. We'll look at the pictures. But I'm quite certain it will need to be treated rapidly." She consents to book into the hospital for the following day. Rebuckling the plaid slacks, she walks away, down the corridor. "She's in bad trouble," Andersson says.

He enters the next examining room reading the chart of a patient unusual for his practice—a sixteen-year-old boy. The boy is taller, even, than Andersson, by nearly half a foot, big-boned, with a wispy red mustache, never shaved, shining on a cupid's-bow top lip. He's oddly long-legged and big-kneed, like a baby workhorse. His dad comes in after him. The boy is a whole foot taller than his father, who is stocky, round-shouldered, with a narrow face. Removing knit tie and yellow dress shirt, the boy reveals the fresh black stitches of a long and recent incision. The track runs from the left nipple, up and around the left shoulder, onto the arm, then halfway down to the elbow. Three weeks earlier, while playing basketball for his high school team, he had suffered what Stearne calls a "purse-snatcher injury." His arm had been swept back by a passing guard so violently that it dislocated. The impact tore apart the major, brachial, artery and also severely stretched the brachial nerve. Andersson had met the boy in the emergency room, and had operated that same night. He knows the boy's father; they're on the bank board together.

"I sewed his artery back together, George"—Andersson addresses the father—"but I could only do so much with the mess I found there."

"Basketball is his life," says the father, looking up at the glorious son, who stands there, inattentive, slack-lipped. "No one realizes better than me the amount this boy has put into basketball in the past seven years. He won't have to stop, will he?"

Andersson has the kindness to address the boy directly. "If you were my son, I'd tell you that you'd never play a contact sport again. You'll understand if you think about this arm in a new way. It is basically a lever to get the hand with that opposable thumb to different places where you will find it very useful. You are lucky to have as much use of it as you do, because when I found you, the arm was dying. There wasn't any blood coming to it. The nerves were damaged. I can't do much about the nerves. I'd have to say no more basketball."

The father frowns, and the boy stares at him now with a

woebegone, frustrated look. The father hands his son back the arm sling he's been holding, and says, "We'll have to put this sling in your trophy case, along with the cups." They both shrug, then smile.

Andersson leaves them to renegotiate their deal with each other. Next room, next chart, next situation, next patient. An old customer this time, a gray-bearded man with the poor hereditary luck to atherosclerose early. Andersson has previously replaced his aorta, given him new femoral arteries in both legs, cleaned out both carotid arteries. He's been on his own for a whole year, and was, in fact, able to work during most of it. "I like my old job—lathe operator," he says. He shrugs. A lot of people in this office shrug. Once more he doesn't feel well. He lies back, unbidden, stripped to gray Jockey shorts, examination gown opened up. Some of the new plumbing—tubes like molehills Andersson has tunneled just below the skin—burrows right across a bulging abdomen. The tubes submerge where thigh joins trunk. The open lapels of his examination gown flap sharply with every pulse beat, flags signaling an alarming blood pressure. His systolic pressure is 150 points high, hovering around 300.

"How do you feel?"

"Fine." The rule around here: Anyone not yet dead, when asked how are you, says fine.

"You're not feeling well?"

"Well, I move slow, I'm foggy. I get confused if I move fast."

"Any other problems?"

"My feet are always cold."

"You're lucky you have feet at all."

The man smiles and looks at Andersson, and says, "Thanks to you."

"Thanks to the Guy Upstairs. I'm just a pair of hands." Andersson says this straight-faced, apparently acknowledging divine guidance. He does sometimes go to church.

"May He always be with you," says the patient.

The man is not fine. Andersson instructs him to walk across

the parking lot, enter the door of the hospital, and sign in with the lady who will be expecting him there. He may call his wife from his room and tell her to bring his bathrobe and toothbrush. The man marches off, resolute. Perhaps he has grown used to this.

Andersson takes a phone call. It lasts only thirty seconds.

"That was the family doctor who sent the lady with the TIA in to me before. She's just died on us." He shakes his head, communicating the surprise and the shame of the loss. She was just here. The density of horrifying melodrama in surgeons' offices overwhelms me, if not Andersson. He stays as detached as a judge at a sentencing. Unlike Stearne, he never lets down his guard, even between patients.

"What happened?" I ask. Andersson just hunches his shoulders. I try a different subject. "How do you feel about the man who was just here?"

"I'm resigned to the fact he'll die young too. He has end-stage circulatory damage from diabetes, and problems with blood pressure regulation. . . ." I push more, asking about Andersson's feelings, probing at least for his discernment of the man's ordeal under these pitiable conditions.

"If I let my feelings surface, I wouldn't be a good surgeon," he says, and shrugs again.

He deals with enough hurting and fear, laid out raw before him each day, to supply a whole team of soap opera script writers. Patient after patient comes to him, betrayed by ill luck and unreliable body. Andersson offers some solace and some help. He seldom offers outright cures, because there seldom are any. Frequently he offers no help at all.

"It's hard to live with. It is. You've got to insulate yourself," he says. He observes symptoms, formulates diagnoses, plans the tactics of treatment. His interest is no broader than that. Patients' experiencing of their illnesses, and their feelings about the surgeon, perhaps at the heart of the human dilemmas here, are of peripheral concern to Andersson—important chiefly for the hints they offer about the disease process. Perhaps he endures only because of his restraint of feeling here. I am haunted

55

with patients' aggregate woe after just weeks of what fills months and years and decades of his life. But even one afternoon is enough to nudge one toward Andersson's attitudes. He says, "Who said it? Satchel Paige? 'Don't look back, someone might be gaining on you.'" Troubles fly by fast. It's sensible to step aside. To assume a functional role. To be professional. To jot down notes of dense-pack action during clinic hours.

Many of the office clocks say 1:30. A. says, "Now we start to roll—faster." And he does. The two tiny panel board examination rooms have racks on outside of doors. Doreen places a patient's record there whenever patient is sent right to examining room without stopping at A.'s office first. This office is well choreographed for production. He touches each patient soon after entering. Rapport. "Hello, young lady," he says to next old woman.

Patient 1: Female, gaunt, thirty, one child. Husband works in mill. Used to work there herself. "The problem is a leg vein," she says. A cosmetic problem. "I was wondering what could be done." Problem looks like a little blue starburst on thigh. He tells her they're not dangerous. "Keep 'em." Says he disapproves of doctors who inject them. "They come back." Scolds her for her smoking, says she'll be back with something serious.

Patient 2, next door: 30-year-old navy officer. Complains of sensitivity of veins in upper thigh. "Seven years ago when I saw you you needed vein stripping. You still do. It's still a purely elective procedure. You're in no danger. Yes, it can be made better. I'm a navy consultant, but they have their own man. Get it done over there."

Patient 3: Old Finn. Concentric oval lines on craggy face. In undershorts. Belly looks laced up—welted scar of recent abdominal surgery. "Aortic aneurysmectomy," says Andersson, pointing. Spirited man, makes self-humbling jokes about being "hardly worth fixing up." He touches Andersson even before Andersson touches him. A pal. Half of his right foot is missing from an old accident. "Your belly's healing nicely."

Patient 4: Electrical engineer, 55. Back pain

radiating into left flank. "Pulses good . . . no aneurysm."
Told he should be followed for the atherosclerosis that
will trouble him later on. Stop smoking.

Patient 5: Foggy, chubby man, retired at 60. Blue
eyes. Ambles across small room, smiling, flaky, half-
undressed, still taking shirt off. Shakes hands. "You're a
pretty relaxed character," says A. "I'm relaxed. I just
can't push when the pressure's on." Has had stroke. Will
get more circulatory tests, as outpatient.

Patient 6: Old man with pacemaker. Gangrenous dot
on middle toe. This is familiar. Pulse exam. Man's foot
pulses gone. Andersson has mimeographed a foot pulse
form for his exam findings. Only checks off a few. Tells
man there's nothing to do. "Keep it clean and raised."
Man goes. A. says he is too old and frail to operate on.

Patient 7: Woman in mid-50s. Blue suede shoes.
Gold-winged glasses. Preppy wool skirt. "My ears ring.
It's a continuing high-toned whistle. Sometimes it cuts off
everything else. I get pulsing from my head to my hand."
Andersson says her sound is called tintinnabulation. Says
he suspects it's high blood pressure causing the ringing,
and thoracic outlet syndrome causing the pulsing. Takes
blood pressure. 220/110. High. It's up recently. Records
from the referring internist show it was 140/70 two weeks
ago. She giggles as Andersson peers into her eye with
ophthalmoscope. "I see nicking in the eye, copper wiring
and silver wiring," he says. Arranges for her
hospitalization, "for further study," he tells her.

Patient 8: House carpenter, 51. Triple chins. Had
heart attack a year ago. Takes hydrochlorothiozide.
Smokes, still, two packs a day. Andersson doesn't say stop.
Two days ago he had terrible pain in "bottom of leg."
Andersson: "Let's go back six months." "I took a long
walk with my wife. I had to stop about eight times. If I
were to dance a couple of dances with my wife, I'd have
to stop." Andersson has him do the "De Weese Walking
Test," stepping in place in his stocking feet, then checks
the blood flow in his buttocks by looking at their color.
Walking should move the blood on down, but it hasn't.

Red buns. Andersson tells him he has "rusty pipes," meaning vessels with plaque in them. "We should think about surgically giving you a new blood vessel to that painful leg. It's a five percent risk of heart attack, stroke, major complications, death. If you don't, it's possible gangrene. . . ." "I'd like to do it right away." That's "informed consent."

Patient 9: Smily ancient lady—all of 90. Pacemaker. She's dressed in green nubbly cloth, like a couch. "You said I could do anything. They've got me singing in a choir now." He checks her pacemaker function, holding a magnet up to her incision line, then a microphone of sorts, then he reads from a computer tape that chuckles out of an adding-machine-like box. Typical tape says: Heart, 70 beats per minute. Pulse width, .8 milliseconds. Amplitude, 5.0 volts. Sensitivity, 2 millivolts. Refractory, 325 milliseconds. Hysteresis, 0 milliseconds. Lead impedance, 420 ohms. Battery impedance, 1 kiloohm. Battery current, 22 microamps. A report from the front lines. Andersson says, "This particular model is doing fine. It's basically a three-year model now." Cryptic. She nods as if she understands. Leaves.

He stops in his office. Dictates notes of the nine cases so far, very fast. Dictation on upholstered lady with pacemaker includes this odd phrase: "Has been notified about possible malfunction of this model pacemaker."

Patient 10: 50-year-old woman in sky-blue suit. Patient of his for six years. She has had phlebitis that developed after she took birth control pills. One of those statistics you read about. Wears tight elastic surgical stockings from heel to upper thigh, all the time. He fits her with new ones. Says, "When the old pair gets loose enough to feel comfortable, you know it's time for a new pair." Fitting device clever. A paper tape measure built like a millipede—many pairs of paper arms dangle from its central spine. He stretches the tape down her leg. The arms are preglued, and Andersson sticks each snugly to its mate, wrapped around the leg along indexed markings. Andersson cuts the tape loose from her leg and mails the whole stuck-together mess in to a manufacturer who will send her stockings along directly, at $100 a pair. She needs four pairs a year. "My insurance won't pay for them," she says, "but they will pay for the surgery that I'll need if I don't use them."

Patient 11: Woman, 79, thin white hair, one squinting eye. Green stretch pants. Big paste pearl necklace. "My doctor thought he heard some sounds in my neck." Operatic voice. Andersson does exam, marking leg pulses on his mimeographed sheet. Feels other obscure pulses, finally, in the neck. Leg pulses poor. He holds her legs up while she lies on table, and times the color change. Says, "Venous fill—fourteen seconds left side, twenty-five on right side." Puts legs down. Puts salve on top of electronic stethoscope and listens. Lady says, in Yankee accent, "I'm built wrong. My nose runs. My feet smell, and I've got *bear* feet, not human feet. Get it?" He applies gooey tip of machine above bridge of her nose. Then listens above carotid arteries on either side of throat with regular stethoscope. He says, "Here's what I find: I think there's a block in one leg artery, a narrowing in the other. Also, your family doctor was right. There is a narrowing in the carotid arteries, here," and he points to neck. "I want to do an aortogram, do a dye test on your circulation. There is a risk. About one person in six hundred has a dye reaction or other trouble. But with your sort of disease, the risk is much higher for not doing anything about it." He makes sure she understands, this time seems slow and kind to a woman in a fix. He offers her a release form, "permitting me to do the procedure," which she signs. He phones the hospital, then tells her, "They have room for you at the beginning of next week—Tuesday morning." She nods, rather sadly.

Andersson dictates notes on the rest of the cases, for patients' files. He says good night to the office staff, and packs the big radio into the trunk of his car. Leaves car parked, and walks across parking lot toward hospital, for evening rounds.

Throughout this afternoon, and again through many others, I am impressed, as I take my notes, by the evenness of Andersson's public disposition. The patients are less consistent. Some, in the most fearsome predicaments, remain sunny and good-natured. Some, with complaints that prove minor or groundless, shake and misspeak, so severe is their anxiety. Andersson side-steps the fear. He goes about his business, slowing down only occasionally to explain procedures to the curious. He uses charts and visual aids—spare pacemakers, unsterile samples of Dacron aortas. For the most part he talks little about what he finds, and still less about how patients should deal with his findings or with their diseases. He has been confronted each day for decades with a few dozen reminders of the unreliability of the body— and therefore of his body—of its mechanicalness, and therefore its fundamental vulnerability. It seems nearly impossible for a surgeon to respond to each of thousands of fearful occasions by feeling frightened, much less by feeling the compassion each situation merits.

Besides, Andersson can help. How strong the temptation must be to become the guardian, to play into the patient's long-ing for omnipotent care, or to back off and join with the well in patronizing the ill. The protective fantasy of personal invulnera-bility, and the desire to be the important doer, the helper, to-gether make it easy. It may go further: a secret inner pulse of exultant sadism can add a thrill and vigor to this insularity. Side by side with death, the chorus of professional helpers sings, "Oh, what can I do to help? Next, please."

And it makes good sense, this kindly and administrative attitude toward suffering. It's self-protective. Lines of patients come complaining to Andersson: "Doc, I hurt." "Doc, I get diz-zy." "Doc, I can't breathe right." What is important to each patient who comes into the office is the knot of subjective feel-ings and private meanings these symptoms have evoked. Andersson forms chords of symptoms out of the cacophony of patients' initial descriptions, then matches them in memory against others encountered during his years of training and ex-perience.

It could be this, that, or the other thing, he thinks. He seeks objective confirmation. Let me see you walk, please. And, I'm going to feel the pulses in your feet. He knows it is not this or that now. It is definitely the other thing. He has treated a thousand cases of the other thing, with fair results. He knows chapter and verse about what can be done. He's up on the literature. The patient's further reports, further complaints, become superfluous. He loses interest, appearing at once less personal.

Then he offers a prediction, to the patient's momentary delight, paying a last visit to this unpleasant world of the patient's subjective experience: "That leg is almost numb—especially in the morning, isn't it?" The patient is ecstatic—she's forgotten to mention that. Yet Dr. Andersson knows. It's as if he shares the pain. A miraculous man. He feels it, and yet he doesn't have it. Protection must be at hand.

But once having determined what he can and can't do, Andersson has little use for a patient's continuing alarmed reports. He stops hearing them. He orders tests. He goes away, and assigns care. Books hospital space and operating time. Moves off to the next examining room to do it over again. Relatives, nurses, technicians, surgical residents take over. Days later, when Andersson next sees his patient, they are both heading for surgery, the one walking, the other riding.

In the course of my time in this world I try to comprehend, and even to imitate for my own comfort, the quality of "professionalism" that protects medical workers from the situations of their seriously ill patients. It turns out to be an easy attitude to assimilate, and one that has some honest pleasures and some naughty thrills associated with it. Healthiness becomes an accomplishment of insiders. It takes little fortitude, after some days of practice, to participate in the seemingly unconcerned banter that wards off lament during the slack moments between patients, the relaxed minutes during the exposing and later the closing of patients undergoing surgery—the same banter Danny

Andersson takes up now, as we walk through the autumn dusk, toward the hospital to check on his patients there.

"Did you hear about the psychiatrist-proctologist combo?" he asks me. "He's a combined specialist in odds and ends." We're both tired. It's a relief to laugh. "And did you hear about the doctor who's writing prescriptions with a rectal thermometer? 'Why are you doing that, Doc?' his nurse asks. He says, 'Oh! I guess some asshole has my pen.'" It begins to rain just before we get into the front door of the hospital.

4

"I'm Perfectly Frank
with All My Patients"

The man in the cranked-up bed in the corner room of the intensive care unit has turned a luminous light blue. As Andersson helps him to sit up, the man's face contorts repeatedly, flickering through a series of expressions—of pain, bewilderment, surprise, and, finally, a suitably public look, a warm smile of greeting. The expressions pass by in seconds, as if caught in a strobe light.

"Hey, Duke!" Andersson shouts.

"Doc!" Duke seems elated, as if Andersson is his lost son, encountered here by chance after years of searching. The warm smile stays on the old lined face. Duke is tiny, a translucent frog. Andersson opens the buttons on Duke's pajamas and inspects a half-yard run of broad stitches that track from belly to pubic bone. He's threaded each stitch through an inch-long crosstie of transparent tubing, giving extra strength to the trussing and sealing in of Duke's new aorta.

"How do you feel, Duke?"

"Doc, hello! I'm fine! You did a great job, Doc! It's so great you come here to see me! Doc!" Duke says it all effusively. Then, looking apologetic, he says, "Doc, I worry. . . ." The flickering gestures replay in sequence.

"I'll give you something. You're doing great, kid. You're

strong." Andersson pats Duke's shoulder. We walk off.

Andersson says to me, "He might make it. He's been through a lot. Threw his pacemaker lead four times. Finally, we went right into his chest and screwed it down. He'd just recovered and then his aneurysm threatens to pop, so in we go again. But what a hell of a nice guy."

I wonder aloud if he hasn't found Duke's effusive gratitude embarrassing. "An animal channel stays open in older patients even when other parts of the mind close off," Andersson answers, "and it asks, 'Does this M.D. care about me?' It's part of the art of medicine to let him know I do. There's a medical value in the aura of doctors—it makes patients willing to listen, do what they must in order to get well. One response to the pedestal bit is to enjoy it. I'm proud I'm a doctor."

We cross the open area of the intensive care unit, passing banks of electronic heart monitors. Andersson has been asked to consult about another doctor's patient. It appears at first that the patient has fled his darkened room, abandoning a heap of brown covers. But he's in there. He barely shows—a tree fallen a few years back that lies covered with mud and leaves. Andersson reaches through the heap of blankets, feeling the patient there as if by chance. He has cancer, and a pacemaker, and now a thrombotic leg.

"How you doing, old fellow?" Andersson asks, peeking into the bog of blankets at a frail, blotchy leg, but not touching it.

"All right."

"Your doctor will see you tomorrow for some tests. Get some sleep." Andersson is out of the murky room in a moment. The man appears to have followed instantly doctor's orders and gone to sleep.

In a small, brightly illuminated room at the opposite end of intensive care, he finds a lady in her seventies, whose long hair is as white as her pillowcase. She sleeps, smiling.

"Mrs. Jones here—we had her carotid opened up yesterday, left side." Andersson points. The carotid area of her neck, left side, is heavily bandaged. "Took out a buildup of plaque. It was ninety-five percent closed. We took that diseased artery, tore hell out of it, beat it up, sewed it up, and it works better than ever. The blood supply to her brain is better than it's been in years."

Unlike Duke, Mrs. Jones doesn't feel up to congratulating the doctor, nor even to moaning. Her color is not good—it's a pallid pinkish gray, once known as "ashes of rose." What happens inside well people is happening outside Mrs. Jones. Sacks of blood, glucose, and clean water mixed with anticoagulant, salts, and antibiotics, all hang from stands above the bed. Secret knowledge of her electrolyte balance, blood count, urine volume, feces weight, are revealed to Andersson, who has removed her red chartbook from the nursing station and brought it with him to the bedside. On a screen above her head, her heartbeat bounces. The boundaries of Mrs. Jones no longer stop at her skin; they fill her room, slip into the rooms of other patients, whose beeping hearts together make an electronic composition of Andersson's devising. His opinion is capital law inside this clean kingdom. He thumbs through the chartbook, locates last night's events, scowls—he finds an incorrect dosage of a drug has been administered during the early hours of morning—shrugs off his irritation, writes up new orders, and lifts Mrs. Jones's limp hand. One eye flickers open, she gasps delicately and smiles a grimace of a smile, higher on the left than on the right. Andersson perceives not a smile, in this crooked gesture, but evidence of slight postsurgical brain damage.

"How do you feel, Mrs. Jones?" A long pause.

"How do you feel, Mrs. Jones?" he asks again.

"Fine," she says eventually.

"Stick out your tongue, Mrs. Jones," Andersson shouts.

Slowly Mrs. Jones receives this idea, decodes it, and resolves to act upon it. But it's a gesture for children, and she can no longer get it right. Her tongue wanders off to the left, chasing her smile, then trembles, retreats between green lips. The mouth stays open; she's fallen asleep.

"She's doing fine," says Andersson.

At the second floor nursing station, Andersson pulls from the circular rack of chartbooks the records of so many patients he must clamp the top of the stack with his chin as he carries it to a desk. He studies each briefly. He takes a few with him on a trek. "These next patients are less ill than the ones in intensive care," he says.

In 201 he greets a spindly old man whose grin stretches back from a set of oversized false teeth. He had a pacemaker installed four days ago. "Young fellow, you look great," Andersson says, leaning and touching the dressing on the chest.

In 206 it's two women, one Irish and one Scottish. The first, fair, fifty, giggly, has ended up here with phlebitis and an ulcerated leg vein. "She's fat, she smokes, and she took the pill—all bad for vascular problems," Andersson has told me. We enter the room. It smells of salad dressing.

"Getting tired of that smelly Burow's solution?"

"Oh, my goodness, yes, Doctor. Hee, hee."

The other woman, older and more retiring, joins the laughter. Andersson feels her leg. "Mrs. MacInnis didn't keep her leg elevated after I did a femoral artery bypass on her. Now she's back," he says.

In 210, "The remarkable Mr. Jefferson. He's lovely, bright, and alert. He has nearly occluded carotids we'll open up, and that's just for starters. He'll do well. He's a sprightly eighty-six." Mr. Jefferson looks pleased.

In 214 he delivers good news. "Frostbite or trashfoot? That's what his GP sent him here for me to find out. Is frostbite bad? Usually not as bad as trashfoot—that's when a blood clot fragments, and ends up in a lot of little shards trapped at the end of the line in the small vessels of the foot." We are ignored by a glum old man sitting in a chair by a made bed, staring up at a television soap opera. "Frostbite's the answer. You can go home today." The patient shows no sign of delight or relief, or, for that matter, comprehension. Andersson just stares at him.

66

"The wife can get me, if you're done," he says eventually, still without looking away from the set.

In 216 a patient sleeps on, whose stitches resemble Duke's, tailored by the same hand.

In 207, an eighty-year-old woman, five days recovered from her second carotid operation, smiles at the doctor and asks, "Will I get prescriptions for the drugs I need when I leave the hospital?"

By the time the evening news from the real world starts to play on patients' televisions, Andersson has peeked at, prodded, stroked, joked with, patted, taken offense at, been stern, fatherly, confidential, and sad with a dozen patients. In the corridor he speaks freely about who will mend, who might not, whom he likes, who annoys him. It turns out to have been impossible to read his true reactions consistently from watching his visits with patients. Yet he often asserts, "I'm perfectly frank with all my patients—hell, they've been around a lot longer than I have."

He settles into a small booth behind the counter of the nurses' station and calls his office, then dictates records into a machine there. He intones complete sentences without expression, and at twice normal speaking speed. "... Could not find evidence to show this was an embolic phenomenon; therefore a discharge. ..." Listening in, I am reminded of the late Cardinal Cushing barreling through the radio rosary with gait so fast and peculiar that only a god, or a skilled secretary, could ever divine its meaning. Then Andersson drives his brand-new Saab home to his wife and children, through a cold rainstorm.

"This is going to be like flaying a whale," Andersson says on his way to surgery at twenty-six miles an hour. He'd gotten half a night's sleep and then his phone rang. A slow emergency—within the hour will do. Now he's squinting into the reddening sky of a chilly dawn, threading through the vacant back streets of a nearby factory town. The slate roofs of wooden tenements have darkened from last night's rainstorm. We arrive, not

67

at the tall main hospital, where he has another patient awaiting surgery at 8 A.M., but at a low brick country hospital with only eighty beds. It has so far resisted the forces closing and combining small hospitals all over the country, because its surgeons do a brisk trade with the tens of thousands of retired workers who stay on, thirty years past the glory days of their half-abandoned mill town. At six in the morning there's no one else in the surgeons' locker room. Andersson is dressed and masked and eyeing the patient in ten minutes.

"This is veterinary medicine," he says quietly to me, then peeks around the operating room after saying it, looking daredevil. A circulating nurse, helping to prepare the patient, has heard. She glares at him. The patient is awake. Perhaps Andersson feels, on too few hours of sleep, the cumulative weight of yesterday's operations and long office hours and hospital rounds. The patient is very fat and also is extraordinarily ugly. Her three-haired chin scoops forward from her face.

Andersson has told me about her. A ward of the government, she's been floated through the public health care system down to this operating room as per order of a doctor at the state mental hospital, because her heart has slowed. It happened during the night. She's eighty-five. Without intervention she will soon die of what one might have thought of, until recently, as old age. She's been in the state hospital for several hearty decades, Andersson has said. Nowadays what she has is not old age, but congestive heart failure, complicated by "heart block," a lessening of the heart nerves' capacity to trigger pumping contractions.

And she can be revived. Andersson is here to install a pacemaker in her. It will sound the depths of her heart and stir its currents. She'll be as good as she was last month, on the ward, before the trouble started. The pacemaker makes a person marvel. This new thing can give years of life. But as great a marvel is the dumb, person-blind system of state health treatment that actually has the kind mandate to deliver care to all patients and has beached this odd woman here, to be fixed up for more life to come.

Three nurses, one of them male and even wider than the patient, tug her from cart to operating table. The male nurse moonlights as an embalmer for a funeral home. Andersson jokes, "Charlie, you here recruiting customers?" Another nurse gloves Andersson's raised hands as he looks past her, at the patient. Awake, but sluggish with discomfort and sedation, the old woman allows herself to be shoved, by sections, onto the table, then taped down, arms extended outward, wrists up, as if she's to be fitted with wings. The funeral nurse backs away from the patient's right arm. Andersson moves into place, examines, momentarily, the configuration of blue wrist veins and spokelike tendons, then cuts down between them to install needle and tubing, through which fluids can pass into her.

I experiment with thinking of her compassionately. "Grandma," I say to myself—I had lovely grandmothers. It doesn't quite take. She's too strange. She does look like the caricature of a hag. She burbles. She even cackles.

Of the hundreds of patients on whom I eventually see surgery performed, she is the only one mad enough not to grasp the proper diplomacy of salvation, and the only one clear-sighted enough, and free enough of politeness and fear, to name what Andersson does to her.

As she feels the point of the knife, she yells: "Hey, cut that out! What the hell you think you're doing?" Andersson goes right on doing what he's doing, and she adds another question, still more sharply framed: "What you think I am?"

An older nurse, in an angry tone, mutters to the undertaker, "If ever I've seen a witch, this is the one." Can the patient hear this too? She is sedated and locally anesthetized but she is not even out cold.

Andersson draws a thin red line with his knife across a hand's width of her chest, over the heart, parallel to the clavicle. He sketches only through skin, on this first pass. Then he draws the knife toward himself again, deepening the line into a trough. It parts behind the blade. He clamps trickles of blood, then ties off these bleeders. A conjurer, he forms stitches from a reel of thread concealed in his palm. The stitches, like small black gnats, crawl from his fingertip every time he snaps thumb against forefinger. They cling to the reddened walls of fat. He takes up the scalpel, holding it with his fingertips, the way one holds a wriggling crab. The knife moves back through the cut again, sunk into the fat below the skin. He ties more bleeders, and abandons the knife in favor of his magical finger.

The finger probes into the incision and then it drives, two joints deep, toward the patient's toes. This is called blunt dissection. The finger swishes back and forth, like a windshield wiper, ungluing a wide pouch of skin from its fastening. He widens the pouch more until it will accommodate three fingers. The pacemaker that will live in the pouch is a little round-edged stainless steel can that resembles a tape measure. It contains a bulk of batteries, and a small circuit board, which ends in a lead socket, implanted in a rubber "boot" that protrudes through the metal case.

Now under very light sedation, her wound dulled by local anesthetic, the patient belches. The funeral nurse laughs. To prevent further enlargement of the incision, Andersson makes two stitches, with prethreaded needles, at its corners. He positions small retractors—they look like foot-long stainless steel hoes—to draw apart the wound's upper and lower lips, and hands the retractors, in turn, to two nurses, who hold the wound open.

He cuts with round-nosed shears, separating anatomy. He digs down into the wound and finds what he knew would be there, the green cephalic vein, wandering back from old brain to weak heart. He works the vein free of surrounding pectoral muscle, then clamps it off and nicks a tiny incision through its side with a scalpel the size of a baby's finger. Into this small opening he threads the first inches of a "lead." It looks like a guitar string encased in translucent plastic, and that's basically what it is—wire wound with Teflon. Each lead costs a few hundred dollars, wholesale. The near end will plug into the pacemaker's lead socket, the far end into the heart. Still kept barely under, the patient grunts, and tries halfheartedly to climb away, then to raise her arm up, at least, to brush the wound. She finds the arm strapped, becomes still, and stares up at the upside down face of the anesthesiologist, a broad-faced Filipino woman, who stares back.

The nurses, the anesthesiologist, and the surgeon pause, and yet another doctor, a radiologist, comes in, heavyset, with brownish bags under his eyes; he is trailed by a female assistant, who looks like a half-sized model of him. The assistant passes out lead aprons, flowered (daisies on a yellow field) for the ladies and solid operating-room blue—the same color as the walls, the surgical drapes, and the floor tiles here—for the men.

Andersson begins to feed more of the end of the lead down into the nick in the cephalic vein, starting it on its path toward the heart. All eyes turn to the television screen above the anesthesiologist's head. On it, amidst pale and darker shadows of organs, dense tissues, and vague arcs of ribs, a black thread slides downward. The tip of this line, snelled like a fishhook with rubbery Teflon barbs, appears. But neither the vein in which the lead first slides, nor the several junctions of vessels to larger vessels, through which the lead passes as it makes its way to the heart, catch the X-rays and show up on the fluoroscope. On the screen it appears that the lead moves freely in the chest. The tip seems to be plotting a course through shadow, past emptiness. The veins are there by inference.

Then the lead tip penetrates the silhouette of the shuddering heart and bangs against the rear wall of the right ventricle, curls back upon itself, and reaches forward and upward for the apical wall of the heart. Andersson, who has piloted this passage with thrusts and twists of the stub of the lead, still showing above the nicked cephalic vein, now gives the stub a final jog. The snelled tip lodges, barbs near the specialized conductive muscle tissue near the tiny "bundle of His," where impulses twitch out syncopated blood pulses. Damage to the bundle of His may be seen directly only during autopsies—it's said to be hard to find even then. The old lady's heart's conduction system is still intact enough to receive the news that the new pacemaker will send.

She has what it takes to go on. Her heart will soon beat as it

71

always has. The fluoroscope screen darkens. "This unit has batteries designed to last seven years, so hopefully we don't have to replace this one ever." The young circulating nurse glares again. The patient appears to sleep.

The lead end now reaches out all the way from the heart. Andersson plugs the free end into the pacemaker, lodged under its pocket of skin. He tears a tiny plastic package and uses a sterile Allen wrench, shipped one per unit, to tighten the tip in its socket.

"Each company sends along a slightly different size of wrench so you'll have to stick with their brand. The other night I was out very late, at a small country hospital where I was called to replace a failing pacer. The fellow's lead was fine. But they didn't have the right wrench, so I had to install a new lead too. You leave the old one right in, next to the new one. It went fine, but the patient shouldn't have to go through the extra wear and tear—and expense. Now I've sent over a set of wrenches and lead adapters for them to keep permanently in stock."

The patient's heart, on monitor, quickens, beeping as insistently as a busy signal, announcing its new strength. Everybody seems to ignore this moment, although arriving at it has obviously been the purpose of the entire exercise. The radiologist's assistant collects aprons. It's like the end of art class. Andersson closes, in a minute or two, the pouch that took fifteen minutes to construct. The room smells sharp and rusty, from medicinal alcohol and blood. "Fastest I ever did this, in a rush, was twelve minutes," he says, tugging on the final stitch.

In the locker room, as we shed surgical greens—his spattered with red—I ask about his feelings of accomplishment. Here he's actually done the trick for a patient—this is one ailment modern science can help and he knows how. He's restored vitality where death would otherwise have ensued.

He shrugs at this indiscretion he's called "veterinary medicine." He does not need to think about it. It's too usual for him. It happens a dozen times a month. This one must offer little further confirmation to his already well-confirmed feelings of accomplishment, powerfulness, and justification. He knots his dull-brown tie, slips on a blue jacket and topcoat, and ascends from surgery. He seems pressed on the subject, though, genuinely puzzled about why he *doesn't* feel prouder—perhaps he suspects he's missing out on a good bet. His shining brow is knit.

As we push out through the hospital's glass front doors, he smiles, the kind of smile he might have come up with as a well-mannered twelve-year-old refusing to tell the answer to a riddle. He hunches up against the chill, says, "I'm just a simple-minded technician," and drives off through wet streets into the sunrise, on to his home hospital and his next customer.

———————◆———————

Some months after her surgery, I tracked down the old woman on whom Andersson had operated. She was back in the state mental hospital, and back in good health. The head nurse on chronic ward 32B told me that she was a darling, a pet, the most affectionate, most cooperative, dear, and helpful patient they'd had there since she didn't know when. The nurse also told me that no, this Dr. Andersson must have been mistaken, that the old lady had not spent her last forty years in the hospital, but had lived quite a normal life—married, had a slew of children, raised them up (they came to visit her all the time, in fact)—had worked in the local factory, been widowed, and only been a patient for a few years. She'd become forgetful at about eighty and needed help, and eventually there was nowhere else for her to go.

The old lady was napping, and awakened to find me sitting by her bed. She decided I was someone she knew as "Paul," held my hand contentedly, and showed me the postcards relatives had sent to her. She'd pasted them on the wall over her bed, in her corner of the ward. And yes, she remembered getting a pacemaker. She patted the scar, and the pink bulge on her chest, and smiled. She was glad to have it. "I was sick," she said.

5

"It Was a Privilege to Raise Him"

We nearly all will be surgeons' customers before we die; we will all harbor disease. We are all their prospective patients. Who are these people, certified by the state to cut us, to plumb secret and fearful places? They regularly do things—cutting, and hurting, and telling bad news bluntly—that, done under other circumstances, would mark the perpetrator as a bully, if not a criminal. They treat, technically and dispassionately, problems that the rest of us fear—cancer, sick hearts, broken bodies. They save lives we are helpless ourselves to save, leaving us beholden to them.

Surgeons' work nearly always makes patients feel far sicker the hour after operations than they were beforehand. Their treatments may well buy time, put the ill on the road to recovery, eventually ease pain. But all that comes later. The first task of the sick body is to recover from whatever the surgeon has done to it. A hundred thousand surgeons do things to sick bodies at the rate of about twenty-five million procedures a year, and get well paid for the work. While healing us, they prosper from occasions of our suffering.

Once taken into the profession, surgeons ally with one another in powerful organizations to protect their privileges and wealth. They limit the quality and number of us who may become like them. They speak to each other in a private language. They have organized themselves as experts, insiders, declared us a public, while controlling an enormous and largely self-regulated cash flow—more than ten billion dollars a year just in direct compensation and many times that amount in money spent on surgeons' authority or at their behest. And as they work, they discuss forbidden topics with each other—death, sex, and their own accomplishment—with the abandon of a huddle of twelve-year-olds. Daily, they have opportunities of a sort most people long to have—to be useful, instrumental, to do things well, to be paid well, and to work within a strong alliance of highly regarded peers.

———————

"Surgeons are a bunch of bastards," Stearne says by way of explaining his trade, "boorish bastards taught by boors—no, no, although that's an old line, and it's pretty close to how I'd characterize them.

"Here. Try this. They're sensitive, caring guys who are completely capable of taking care of people. They are able, doing types, full of vitality and energy, and they like to take action.

"You've heard the story about the GP, the internist, and the surgeon? They go duck hunting. They make a bet. The guy who shoots the first duck gets his dinner bought by the other two. But if anyone shoots a bird that isn't a duck, he pays the other two a hundred bucks. A flock of birds comes over, and the hunting starts. The GP says, 'There's a bird—it looks like a duck . . .' and finally he gets off a shot at it. The internist says, 'There's a bird—it looks like a duck . . . gee, maybe not . . . well, maybe yes, I'm not sure . . .' and by then it's too late to pull the trigger. Meanwhile, the surgeon says, 'There's a bird,' and *bang* goes his gun. As the bird is falling, he says, 'I hope it was a duck.'"

Danny Andersson, in a similar discussion, a few months after the Atlanta surgeons' congress, in his office across the breadth of New England, says similar things about his colleagues: "Surgeons are package people. When I am presented with a sick gall bladder, I will pluck it out, and if you don't get better, that's an affront to me. I am introspective: Whenever something doesn't happen the way it should, I ask myself, 'Am I doing all that I can to help this patient as much as they can be helped?' If the answer is yes, I'll sleep soundly even if the patient isn't doing well. No quality physician can separate himself completely from patients. But you learn to be objective.

"Surgeons are nice, sweet guys—no, seriously. They may not be interested in who you are personally, as the family doctor is. They concern themselves with the package: Here's a problem; let me solve it and go on to something else. They're willing to work longer hours than colleagues. Not interested in primary care—the earaches and sore throats. They don't delve deeply into the patients because they don't want to—or are afraid to. A bit more callous about some disease patterns than other doctors are. Cardiac and vascular surgeons die earlier than other specialists, even other surgeons. But surgery—that's where you can really change things, make things better, save lives, prevent heart attacks, strokes. Or you may maim, cripple, kill. Maybe it's the macho business—entering the inviolate. Maybe that's why we die younger."

Both Stearne and Andersson share impressions of surgeons as "men of action," "impersonal," "technically deft," "divorced from the emotional content of the work," and "more direct than other sorts of doctors." These stereotypes, which seem to be shared by TV writers and many patients, are also confirmed by the work of social scientists studying surgeons. A few sociologists and physicians have undertaken studies that correlate personal characteristics with choice of medical specialty. A persistent social scientist named Henry Wechsler sorted through these studies and put their findings together in two pages of his *Handbook of Medical Specialties*, which I paraphrase here, omitting the many footnotes but sharing some of the handbook's language:

Surgeons have been mostly males, and mostly come from families with many brothers. A high proportion went to public colleges, and had fathers and brothers who were doctors too. Only some have done remarkably well in college; three studies on the subject contradict each other. One reported that surgeons had low grades as medical students, another said surgeons' grades were evenly distributed throughout their classes, and a third, that surgeons were the best students.

Surgeons have been found to be most firmly set, while in medical school, about their career choice. Studies of surgeons' emotional lives reveal a group with things well in hand: studies find surgeons low in neuroticism, low in anxiety about death, low in depression and nervous tension. They show men able to handle taxing emotional situations without distress, with thick skins, with self-confidence.

Surgeons are described by researchers as extroverted, easygoing, "oriented toward people," emotionally expressive, and easily pleased (the last ought to worry any prospective patient). "They are not very reflective and have little tolerance for ambiguity," are authoritarian, stubborn, believe in the doctor's authority and need for controlling dealings with patients. They are practical, realistic, not very "concerned with establishing warm and friendly relationships with patients," because such psychological skills seem to them less crucial to healing than do the technical ones. They don't value rapport with patients highly, nor "the psychosocial aspects of medicine," and feel "less bound by traditional roles of conduct" than other doctors do.

Surgeons score high on tests measuring aggression, dominance, endurance, perseverance, cynicism, compulsiveness, and memory for facts and details. They score low on need for introspection, emotional support, humanitarianism. They trust logic above feelings, aren't very interested in aesthetic and cultural concerns, and are good at and interested in handling tools, materials, and machinery.

"Finally, a high percentage of surgeons-in-training expected to earn a high income and tended to give great weight to the recognition and opinions of colleagues."

This sometimes contradictory dose of social scientists' wisdom, representing dozens of studies, stops at the office door.

There's nothing personal about the findings, of course; they reflect an actuality of aggregates, not of humans in particular—not Stearne, not Andersson. But surgeons seem so often to embody the aggregate type to other hospital workers that the term "surgeon's personality" commonly communicates something akin to the findings—an egotistical, emotionally cold, vain, and skillful technician. Nurses at both Andersson's and Stearne's hospitals confided in me that each man has "a real surgeon's personality."

Some of the shared impression of surgeons may reflect both the anger and deification that we invest in persons who cut other persons artfully. But over the long haul it seems unlikely that a mere human can work with responsibility for and authority over the wounding and repair of patients without manifesting egotism, vanity, and aloofness. "Surgeon's personality" goes with the territory. The circumstances of the job would seem to invite practitioners to develop whatever of these traits they lacked when they first chose the work.

"All disease involves intelligible physical transformations of processes and systems," Andersson once explained, "even diseases for which the transformations take place on a molecular scale." Then he added, "When the trouble is big enough to attack with a knife, I do all I can." It was a candid and striking assertion, a surgeon's explanation of his sense of mission, a heady conjunction of out-and-out aggression and saintliness—"attack with a knife" meets "do all I can." To wound in order to do good seems a particular and remarkable sort of occupation to wander into, and surgical rotation either repels or beguiles medical students considering the prospect of a lifetime of repeatedly reenacting this formulation of saintly aggression.

———————

In his office, while drawing the map that would lead me northward to his parents' home, Danny Andersson had impeached the witness in advance. He seemed worried about my impending conversation with his father. "My father changes things from what they were," he'd said. I drove north for hours, to hear about the surgeon as a boy. Dreadfully short of breath because of emphysema, wearing a red dressing gown and sitting among Chinese antiques in his glass-walled living room in far northern New England, Andersson's father appeared, for all his illness, ageless and built very much like his son.

Mr. Andersson: "From the time he was four or five, without my prompting, Danny said he wanted to be a surgeon. The first toy I ever saw him really fret to get was a toy stethoscope.

"He stumbled on his way to visit a friend, crossing the tracks at age six. He cut his arm on glass. His mother heard him yell, from far away, 'The bleed! The bleed!' as though he were afraid. We took him to a doctor, who stitched him and then tried to give him a tetanus shot. Danny panicked. The doctor could not manage to give it. Finally, he turned the syringe over to Danny and said, 'I'm not afraid, you know. You give me the injection first.' Danny was surprised. He stopped crying. 'I couldn't do that,' he said, and gave the syringe back. Then he didn't yell. And it was the same doctor who gave his first dissecting kit to Danny when he went off to medical school."

It's a sweet old story, about a kindly deception, an ironic offer to turn over the instrument of aggression. Danny Andersson's father's next story turned out to be a repeat of the previous one. Mr. Andersson, after a moment's recollection, spoke of his son's mildness and obedience. "He never caused us one bit of trouble, ever," he said, shaking his head to emphasize this steadiness. I asked if Danny had *ever* acted up.

Mr. Andersson: "Well, there was one time. He was eleven or twelve. He talked back to his mom. But that I wouldn't take. 'Danny,' I said, 'we're going to your room.' When we got there I took off my belt. It was a belt with a heavy buckle. I handed it to him. I said, 'I must have been a lousy father to bring up a boy who'd talk back. So beat *me*, and use the buckle end. 'Oh, no! I couldn't do that!' Danny said to me. And I said to him, 'All right, then, apologize to your mom. You have a lot to make up to her.' He ran ahead, and when I got into the room, they were sobbing and hugging each other."

I thought I could imagine why young Danny was sobbing and hugging his mother. I'd have been relieved to have gotten out of there; he must have been overwhelmed by his father's frightening, ironic invitation to do something it would be folly for the boy to go ahead and do. Twice in consecutive tales, the horrified Danny answers, in the memory of his frail old father, "Oh, no! I couldn't do that!"

But why was Mrs. Andersson crying? Was she simply touched by Danny's contrition? Was she appalled at her husband's maneuver, and thinking to herself: Oh, no, he's doing it again? She remembers the episode, she later told me, but not any tears of her own. "We never had any more problems from Danny, and nobody used the belt. It was a privilege to raise him."

The making of a surgeon may begin with incidents such as these, which turn fury into self-sacrifice. Thirty-five years after the event, Andersson does not remember the belt episode at all.

———

Andersson's mother had a weak constitution, and spent much of Danny's boyhood either in a hospital or home in a hospital bed. Her lungs were weak. Danny liked her doctors.

Danny's father had almost become a doctor himself. As Mrs. Andersson tells it, her husband had gone through two years of medical school at Harvard, in the early 1930s. Then, during a school break, he and a close pal went west on the railroad. The train wrecked during a rainstorm. Danny's dad stood in an open field by the tracks, next to his friend. A lightning bolt struck the friend, killing him.

Back at Harvard, during a surgical demonstration in an amphitheater, Mr. Andersson said, he had "frozen" when the professor addressed him. He took time away from medical training, and never went back to it. In the end, he spent a long career as a middle-level bureaucrat in a large bank, where he specialized in pension fund management. According to his son, he was always comfortable, and never wealthy.

Early on, Danny Andersson became committed to the idea that he would study medicine himself. His maternal aunt, a doctor, encouraged the choice. His parents were of the do-it-himself school of educational funding. They told him so and, as his mother put it, "to see him work, as a boy, at odd jobs, with his goal so clearly in mind, was inspiring."

Andersson's father offered a further recollection of his son's dutifulness. "When the boy was eleven, his mother had an accident, cutting herself badly when she broke a crock of mincemeat for Thanksgiving pies on the edge of a Monel metal counter. I heard her faintly calling, 'Daddy, Daddy.' I called Danny and said to him, 'Son, it's bloody, but you have to help her. Did Cub Scouts teach you about pressure points?' 'Yes,' he said to me, 'but I don't remember.' He remembered, but he wanted to make sure. I showed him where to keep his thumb, count to twenty, let it out, do it again. I got my wife's coat and phoned the doctor. It was early morning.

"We got back hours later, because she'd needed stitches. We'd eaten no breakfast. As we came up the walk I saw the curtain on the front door move. It was Danny. He'd darted away from the window when he'd seen us coming, and gone to turn on the stove. He'd cut grapefruit. He was scrambling eggs and making toast when we walked in. He'd gotten cold water, salt, and taken the blood out of the rug. There wasn't a sign of it. Not a sign."

Danny's dutifulness had turned more to medical matters by high school. His mother recalls his first work in medicine. "He got a summer job as a flower girl in a hospital—I mean he delivered flowers to patients and pushed them around—I mean wheeled their beds. There was a taxi accident on Fifty-seventh Street. Danny saw it. He was on his way from his aunt the doctor's to the job. Maybe it was a trolley. The driver was hurt. It wasn't far enough for an ambulance. The hospital doorman went with a cart and an intern to get the patient. The driver's leg had been severed. They loaded the driver onto the cart. Danny picked up the leg; he was not agitated. 'I wasn't going to leave it there,' he told me that night, and I wasn't sure if he was making it up. But when he said, 'I was surprised I could do it,' I had to believe him." Danny's mother's thoughts, lodged on the subject of accomplishment, leapt to a new topic with no pause: "His father has a Ph.D. in English from Harvard, except he had to apply for it and he never had the five hundred dollars because he was paying for his sister's medical school at the time."

Danny went off to prep school, to better qualify himself for the medical life. "While in public school, Danny sat on his fat back porch and brought home beautiful grades," his father had said. In prep school, presumably off his porch, Danny also did well, and while doing well, earned his own way. Other boys squired dates to the prom, his mother remembers with pride, but he hired himself out to take pictures of the dancing couples. And once on the subject of photography and accomplishment, her thoughts again leapt: "He and his dad bought me a pair of perfume bottles. Danny photographed it so beautifully. He caught the facets of it. We realized, way back when he was fourteen, that he was doing great work. I didn't think he was brilliant—and I still don't. His dad is. His wife learns things easier. He was always mad at his wife for that."

During his last year at the prep school, Danny went to Harvard for an interview, to the school that had yielded his father neither M.D. nor Ph.D. He came home and sat down with his mother and said to her, "It's too big for me." He interviewed across town, at Tufts, and ended up going to college there.

"Danny had to find his own place to live there," his mother recalls, "and he did. There were rows of wooden buildings. Firetraps. I resented that; I left crying, but I didn't let him see it. He met his wife there. After six months as a freshman, he was teaching biology. She was one of his students. A week after he met her, he called me and said, 'Mother, I met a little redhead. She's like you.' Why, she's no more like me than the man in the moon. She's effervescent. She's full of ginger."

Danny was to interview again at Harvard. During his final year at Tufts, he returned to look over the medical school. He found reason to get angry at what he took to be a distasteful comment by his interviewer, and got up out of his chair and left the interview in the middle. He was accepted at another medical school, farther west, and settled down to figure out finances, and love, and anatomy.

He sent a note home to his mother just before Easter that said, "You're going to get a package in the mail. It may smell. Keep it out of doors where nothing will get at it." It arrived, and sure enough, it did smell.

Danny arrived home shortly after his package. He found that his mother, ever supportive, had bound more strings around it and hung it out the attic window. He unwrapped it, revealing a dead cat.

He boiled the cat in his mother's canning kettle, set on a hot plate in the backyard. He dried the bones. He had a talk with his mother, and signed her up to help. Then, throughout the school holiday, the two of them worked on resurrecting it. They set out all the bones on a sheet on the living room floor, and they drilled holes and threaded fine wires between the joints. When it was done, the cat skeleton was so well articulated, "you could move it like it was alive," Mrs. Andersson remembers. "It was wonderful." Returning to his studies with it, Danny presented it to the college, and, says his mother, "Twenty years later, they still display it, or did until the building it was in burned up."

In medical school, Andersson worked long hours. "I wasn't the best in the class, but I did quite well, and I worked at it. I'm not a brilliant mind; my father was," he says. He married the "cute little redhead," and she supported them through some lean years of study.

When he first went to set up in practice in New England, he left his wife and young children living near his medical school. He bought a used examining table, repainted a small office himself, and "slept on my desk." He performed the acts of political deference needed to break into his new town's round of referrals: "I called on the established doctors, and drank coffee until it came out my ears. I took the cases they sent me gratefully—and at first, a lot of them were the cases that involved difficult patients, or that had to be handled on weekends or holidays." After a few months, Andersson's wife was able to join him. "I vowed never to move, and I haven't," he says.

Does Andersson's tame and dutiful boyhood square with the social scientists' portrait of a surgeon? This man's delight seems to lie precisely in his fulfillment of the role, not in his uniqueness. He's happy at it. He likes being the surgeon who is needed; being in role has become "being himself." When a man's work traffics in life and death, is it any wonder that after a time the role and the man can't be separated? To the extent that their senses of "self" emerge from their work, and not the unique personalities who happen to be doing this work, surgeons march out of cadence with this age of individualism.

6

"My Experience with This Kind of Complication Is Pretty Limited"

Stearne, in a green-webbed lawn chair, in the greenhouse off the kitchen of his ark-on-a-hill, measures the progress of Sunday in spent sections of the *Times*. He's done with "Sports." "The Week in Review" lies on top of it, on the gravel floor, and in the next half hour he tosses the two parts of the first section, beginning with the day's wars and ending with its marriages, on top of that. Stearne has read well into the business section, checking the advances and declines of certain stocks. His black hair gleams in the sun. Light reflected from the shining green leaves tints his face. The buzzer on his belt goes off, a thin piping of the local news that downtown, a recent disaster is being organized for treatment by him.

Stearne rises slowly out of his chair. He calls the hospital. Then he calls his partner, Culver, who is also at home. He does not waste time, but neither does he leave at a sprint. He is not excited by emergencies. They interest him. They are part of his routine, to be handled with decorum, not frenzy. He says good-bye to his wife. Within five minutes of the beeper's announcement, he is in the Mercedes. Another five minutes of rather fast driving, down the twisting hill to town, and he's in the hospital's reserved parking lot.

Sundays, hospitals shut down as much as they can. The few

true surgical emergencies that come in are as likely to require an orthopedist to set broken bones as they are a general surgeon. This emergency involves no broken bones, but rather a torn circulatory system that is emptying itself. The patient, her life leaving her, is still conscious as Stearne walks into the emergency room. He greets the head nurse. She takes him back to the patient, a woman of about sixty, who lies on a litter, ready to travel, but still half-clothed. She herself is a retired nurse, flaccid-faced, waxen, and glassy-eyed. Her medical knowledge has given her a chance to survive. Ten years earlier, according to her chart, she had had a nylon artery installed in place of her own ruined aorta. No one uses nylon anymore. This morning, the wall of her prosthesis, where silk stitches holding it in place had come in contact with the intestines, must have worn through—at least that's what the doctors here were guessing. In her closed body, at the top of the abdomen, just below the fastening of the nylon prosthesis to the stump of the old aorta, seepage must have begun. The symptoms had seemed slight to her at first—just a fullness and mild abdominal pain. It could have been indigestion. But the nurse had read her own signs and understood something. She had driven herself to the hospital. There she grew rapidly worse. She's in shock now.

The rituals of surgery usually begin a day ahead of time, and proceed with the deliberateness of a countdown for a space launching. Elaborate bathing and bowel-emptying purgatives occupy the patient. Operating room preparations also start far in advance of surgery, also with elaborate, almost ceremonial, cleansings, with the packing of carts with kits of instruments, with the gathering up of special supplies, with the assembling of appropriate paperwork. The anesthesiologist stops by the evening before the morning of the event, to take the measure of the patient and then plan dosages.

This time, aides wheel the sick nurse into the operating room within moments after Stearne's arrival. They bump a recently scheduled appendectomy; he will go on waiting, drugged and dozing in the corridor, for a few hours.

Stearne scrubs for two minutes instead of ten. The nurses

help insert intravenous catheters in the patient's plump white arms in the same few minutes, accomplishing deftly the fussy chores that sometimes take them half an hour. The anesthesiologist has the patient under in moments, and begins preparing bags of blood for transfusion. Stearne walks in, scrubbed, and the patient is ready. As Stearne makes the first cut through the still damp skin of the broad orange-swabbed belly—cutting less delicately than he usually does to enter bellies and in fewer installments—Culver walks in, smiling and pushing his hands into gloves.

Stearne cuts deeper. The clotted seepage from the torn aorta, suddenly freed of the pressure of the gut, tumbles into the abdomen, which Stearne is still opening. In a moment, the clean, deepening incision is a sump of black blood. Ropes of clot swirl in it.

"I hope that blood is available for transfusion already," Stearne says. The anesthesiologist nods. Stearne sounds nervous. "She's had a lot of previous surgery here. She's been open three, four times before. I hope the last guy left the renal artery out of the way." He works fast. He seems pure and concentrated, exempt from the burdens of his complex nature. Before planning just how to repair the aorta, he must expose the entire eroded area. He has to look at it. And blood is coming into the wound more quickly than he can pump it out with the one aspirator that's been set up. The transfusion isn't going yet. The nurse is in deep shock, and near to dying. Only so much blood can leave the system before pressure drops and the heart, with too little to pump, disorganizes and arrests.

Surgery is seldom like this. Most of the millions of procedures done by surgeons each year are elective, deliberate, and come and go with no moments of crisis at all. With the institutionalization of anesthesia more than a century ago, surgery became rather unhurried. There's still a tradition that speed counts—it goes back to the days when surgical patients were held down, screaming, as the work progressed. Hours do still count; general anesthesia is hard on the body. And busy surgeons may work quickly so they can perform more operations in a day. But surgeons nowadays take care, rather than saving minutes, whenever there's a choice between the one and the other. There's no choice now.

Things get worse. Stearne is feeling through the anatomy of the upper abdomen with his hands submerged. He lodges retractors behind the intestines and has nurses pull the gut back out of the way. The blown prosthesis fragments further. It excretes a clot the size of a baby's fist, which floats up into view. Blood floods the widened incision. "It's just ruptured," Stearne says. His hands are under blood to the wrists. He can't see. Too much time is passing. At least the transfusion has now started flowing. Stearne says something now so tame, so unpreening and frank, that it seems endearing: "My experience with this kind of complication is pretty limited."

It would be a rare surgeon, this side of a battlefield tent, whose experience with this kind of complication was not pretty limited, for patients whose prostheses let go nearly always bleed out in moments, and do so wherever they happen to be, which is seldom on the operating table, where help may save them. It's not a bad way to die.

Stearne has trouble finding surgical landmarks in the murk. He's having trouble even finding the mouth of the flow so he can clamp it off, sorting blindly through the chaos of adhesions and clot. Someone dumps saline solution into the wound. The blood marbles, then reddens again. Culver reaches into this wash, feels, then finally nods and says, "Yup." He has located the aorta's upper stump. He folds his hand down onto it. Stearne picks up a large arterial clamp—called a "Cooley," after Denton Cooley, one of the pioneers of cardiac surgery. It must be a height of manly success to have the only tool that can do the trick in crisis moments named after you. Cooley enters, from two thousand miles away, when nothing less will do.

Stearne follows the line of Culver's wrist and thumb with his own hand and forces the clamp under the sunken stub of artery. A surgical nurse gets a second aspirator organized and, finally, blood begins draining from the wound. The play of hands and the prodding clamp come into view. The flow is under control.

"If I can just get around completely, I can get the clamp secure on this," says Stearne. Under ordinary conditions, "getting around" the aorta with the clamp would have been accomplished deliberately, set up even before blood flow in the artery was interrupted. Only Culver's folded hand, thrust into the abdomen, keeps the unconscious woman's remaining blood in her now. The patient's dropping blood pressure steadies on the red digital meter by her head: 57, 59, 58, 70, 80, it flashes.

"Things are so mixed up here," Stearne says, "I can't tell for sure if I'm feeling plastic or artery." He thrusts with the Cooley clamp in his right hand and cuts, tentatively at first, with scissors in his left.

"I've got this O.K.," says Culver. "It looks like you're up far enough so it ought to be the real thing, not scraps of the old prosthesis."

"There, I've got it clamped." Everyone sighs, almost in unison.

"Syringe," Stearne says. A heavy-set nurse, hands him a giant syringe with a rubber bulb on the end. He draws up a cylinderful of blood, hands it back to the nurse, who squirts it into a bowl and throws in the new graft she is preparing. Things are looking up. They're thinking of finishing this operation.

"This is still spraying—I've got it clamped but we're still losing blood," Stearne says to Culver. He sounds freshly alarmed. "If this clamp is on the shreds of the old graft after all, and not back on the real aorta, and it blows above it along the old suture line, we're in real trouble because I can't get more room to reclamp any higher."

Stearne probes more. The aspirator finally drains to the floor of the wound. He can see into its whole depth.

"It's O.K. It's high enough," Culver says. Stearne has his sense of location now. He slides another arterial clamp in and fastens it quickly, just below the first. The spraying stops. He and Culver clean up. They lift from the wound strands of blood clot and cracker-sized sheets of the "neointima" that must have formed inside the blown-out prosthesis. "Yiich," says Culver. They cut away at the top of the old prosthesis.

"There," says Stearne. "There's the ring of the proximal aorta, clear of junk." It's a red, fleshy cross section of tube, craggy and rough-edged. "It's like cement inside, and lousy tissue outside."

"Maybe you can clip away at it and clean it out?"

"May I have a right angle?" Stearne asks the nurse. He reaches into the aorta and fishes out more clot. He probes farther. "The back wall of it is pretty much eroded"—more prodding—"but we may have enough to work with."

Inches below the patient's pumping heart, he tidies the ring of the aorta, shearing it back to tissue stable enough to hold the stitches that will tie in the new prosthesis.

Culver opens the incision into the belly still further, neatens it up, and then inspects the lower section of the torn graft. He clamps off its two iliac legs. Stearne decides he will preserve them. He cuts the loosened old graft away just above the iliac clamps. The new graft will join to good aortic tissue at the top, but onto these nylon cuffs at the bottom. They're still sound. This will allow a smaller incision and a briefer operation. The patient has been through a lot.

Slowly, Stearne builds order. He resets the retractors to open the territory. He displays—framed and suspended by clamps—the stubs of aorta and of both graft legs. The impeccable organization he imposes crowds away the bloody mess in this belly and promises more life. Stearne again seems calm. It seems to occur to him now that he has appeared—however appropriately—timid for a time, and that he has accepted encouragement, and even valuable help, from Culver. He works on, lighthearted and bold now, and his talk seems to flow from such a realization.

"Charlene, would you keep your boobs out of the way?" he says to the white-haired nurse next to him. She doesn't answer, she doesn't move, and she doesn't smile. "I don't mind," Stearne says, "they're so soft and nice." Then he asks the anesthesiologist, "How you doing, Sid?"

"Pretty good."

"Why don't you ask me how I'm doing?" Stearne asks everyone present. He seems to reflect as he cuts and sews. "The hero is the assistant, who has to stand around for three hours, watching," he says.

"I urge him on," Culver says. Combat's behind them now.

"The urine output has increased," the anesthesiologist reports, doing his job.

"The patient's or Dr. Stearne's?" Culver asks.

Stearne smiles behind his mask.

Stearne's alliance with Culver is no oddity. Joined by the strain of dangerous service together, surgeons in partnership become as tight as cops in the same patrol car. Their loyalty to one another, as each other's most expert aide and witness to each shared venture, may in time exceed their feelings of obligation to any passing patient. One should not get second opinions about impending surgery from partners, or even acquaintances, of one's surgeon. In rough moments, partners help and empathize with each other; afterward, they may explain away each other's misadventures.

In Stearne's city, most of the surgeons who operate regularly have assisted each other at least a few times over the years, during operations that regular partners could not attend. Such alliances are imperfect—factions, and grudges abound. Surgeons have long memories and ample pride. Few surgeons take the ability of their colleagues on faith. Denton Cooley has been quoted as saying, "A successful surgeon should be a man who, when asked to name the three best surgeons in the world, would have difficulty deciding on the other two." But if the rivalry between surgeons is extreme, perhaps the most obvious cause is commercial: one surgeon's patient is another surgeon's lost business. There's not quite enough to go around. All surgeons can prosper; few work as hard as they might. Surgeons say vicious things about other surgeons, but only after choosing their audiences with care. One never bad-mouths a surgeon to his patient. But surgeons know each other's worst moments. And most surgeons have in common a scorn for bad craftsmanship.

This paradoxical familiarity turns out to make surgeons mutually vulnerable and, finally, makes them all allies. They're in it together. Locally, they can implicate each other for not being perfect. Everyone's committed a few errors in his years of practice. On a national scale, surgeons have joined together in a professional and political alliance that has almost crowded non-surgeons out of the operating room (although some rural GPs still do tonsils and appendixes). Their organizations lobby to control both the licensing of foreign-trained surgeons and the numbers of surgeons trained each year here in America.

But beyond the shared vulnerability, and the commercial advantages of a national alliance, surgeons share a world. They share a proprietary feeling of competence, of responsibility, of unlimited aspiration, yet of frustratingly limited capability tested daily in crucial episode after crucial episode. "There is no minor surgery," almost any surgeon will get around to saying. Only other surgeons share the assumptions and memories of this odd life, whose functional moments take place inside other, sleeping, trusting people.

The alliance seems most obvious in the surgeons' dressing room at Stearne's hospital, at the far end of the six-operating-room surgical corridor. The younger surgeons, in scrub suits, crowd around each other for a few moments now and then like boys at a pajama party, while down the hall nurses prepare patients, or wheel them in or out of surgery. Stearne can't share his everyday world so fully with any other group. Its premises are too odd, and the only others who belong have endured the same ordeals of danger-by-proxy, and the touching of the sick places where life is hidden, held, and lost. Like the students staring at the corpse in the print of Rembrandt's *Anatomy Les-*

son that hangs in Stearne's office, stand together, in the thick of things.

———————◆———————

Having seen the retired nurse settled in the recovery room next door, Stearne joins Culver in the dressing room. It could be a dressing room for a private gym—white-tiled, full of blue lockers. They make small talk about Culver's ten-speed bike. Culver likes to go on hundred-mile rides. A burly gynecologist comes in. His operating suit is drenched from the waist down with pale-pink ooze. Stearne shouts out, in greeting, "Heinrich, you've been swimming!" It seems cavalier at first thought, and consoling at second. The dressing room is their senate cloakroom, officers' mess, men's club library. It's where, while changing clothes in front of each other, surgeons consult on fine points, share combat stories of surprises recently found in patients; where they trade righteous accounts of frustrating dealings with nurses and hospital administrators; where, summers, they tell each other tales of an endless, jointly played round of golf.

Samurai meeting here between battles, surgeons sustain each other in ways they'd be reluctant to acknowledge. They seem to tolerate, even to admire, in each other the very proudness and self-absorption that others in the hospital refer to when they complain about "surgeons' personality." If such self-absorption condemns most surgeons to lifetimes of hard work, bonhomie, stiff bravado, and clubbishness but little intimacy, it also may make the daily onslaught of carnage endurable. It must be very gratifying indeed to be on the team that can rescue persons.

———————◆———————

In street clothes, Stearne stops once more in the recovery room to see his patient. Then he drives back up the hill home, and resumes his place in the lawn chair in the greenhouse. He reads the *Times Book Review* for a while. I ask about the operation he's just finished. My technical questions he answers with aplomb. Questions about his moments of seeming timidity and bewilderment he waves aside. And when I ask if he feels proud of himself, and if his alliance with Culver, comforted him this afternoon, he stops me.

"I'm not much for introspection. It's like peeling the petals from a rose," he says.

"A *rose?*"

He reflects, then looks sheepish, a boyish smile playing on the small features of his chubby, angelic face. "Maybe not like a rose. Like an onion, maybe," he says. "Anyway, I don't do much introspection. In fact, I avoid it. I avoid it as a function of the human creature. I wouldn't step out the door in the middle of winter without dressing up warmly. It's cold out there and I'd quickly be uncomfortable." He holds out a hand, palm up, being reasonable. "It's the same way with all this stirring things up. I function very well as I am. I wouldn't want to disturb things. Sometimes when I'm up in the middle of the night, scenes do play back, but I don't take note of them so I remember them afterwards, and I don't know how to get into that state."

The onion's hard to peel. The sun slants in from the far side of the greenhouse now. The kids play in the kids' wing and not on the lawn. Cats prowl about. A new puppy howls from its cage in the big living room. Stearne remembers his boyhood.

"I know what my kids are doing. I was allowed to come and go from the age of six—I was the eldest and I used to take my mother's ration book to the store and do the shopping. One day I lost it, and stayed by the store for hours, searching for it. Perhaps my home was too loose. That was a lot of responsibility for a little kid. I don't ever recall my parents telling me not to do something. My parents didn't provide much of a family structure. My dad worked all the time. We kids provided our own, more or less. A home with that many kids—there were five more after me—all the authority absorbs into itself. From when I was thirteen until sixteen or so—maybe it was me and maybe them—I got quite alienated from the household for a while. My conflicts at home absorbed a great deal of my energy in those teen years. The rest was taken up by school—and cold showers."

In between cold showers, Stearne raised hell backward. He recalls only a single straightforward incident of raising hell frontways—just cutting up the way most free-spirited Catholic school lads of seventeen might. "It was thirty years ago. I don't remember it too well. We tried to get served in New York City—a bunch of us went down there. Someone had a car. And there was this other time . . ."

He continues, but the other time turns out not to count. It's a time he wishes he'd cut up, but hadn't, when the genius of alcohol kept him honest: "I went up to Harvard for my interview. I had a friend up there from my town, older than me. I stayed with him. He served me icebox martinis from the refrigerator in his dorm room. We were with some girls from Radcliffe. They watched, shaking their heads as I spilled a few down, one right after another. They looked at me strangely. Then we all went out. I don't remember much else—just that I spent most of the evening in alleys, looking at the wall and heaving."

This night of Radcliffe girls and drink was alien to his earlier childhood. His usual impulse seems to have been, then, just what it is now—to rebel not by fooling around but by heroically defying others' limited expectations of him. "There aren't big incidents in my childhood. I channeled my aggression into doing well at school. I had the sense that doing well was showing them."

"Them" meant not just parents but priests. Stearne says, wistfully, "Once a Catholic, always a Catholic. Like all Catholic surgeons, I think abortion is morally wrong. Even were I not a Catholic, I wouldn't do them anyway—except if my daughter needed one. . . ." He pretends to look shocked at himself, then laughs.

Stearne's mother had climbed out her bedroom window at

eighteen and eloped. "She was a banker's daughter, and she ran off with a working-class boy—my dad says he finished high school, but he didn't. My dad is self-made. You know how he made it? He made it through golf. He was a caddie, and as good as a semipro golfer when he married. He worked as a stockboy at a big department store. Because he was so good, he played with store executives. One day one of them asked him what he aspired to in his work. "Fifty dollars a week," he answered. He was earning five at the time. Eventually, he became their buyer in the area of women's underwear, and he learned the business. After the war he became vice-president of a brassiere company. At fifty-six he was out on the street, though, because of a merger. He contacted some Chinese backers and started importing clothing from Taiwan. He's a wheeler-dealer. He has a cabin cruiser he loves. Polishing it all the time. I was never close to him. He was always out, and he worked Saturdays.

"What kept me in line was Catholic school; I am the child of a parochial-school education. The priests wanted the top kids to join their order. Four of the top six in high school did. They work on you. They take you aside. I was on the rifle team—how's that for channeled aggression? Rifles? Get it? But the priest who was coach gave me constant doses of Thomist philosophy—the Good, the Beautiful, the True, which according to them are the aspirations of the human soul. I wonder if they are. The other top kids were placed in leadership positions. I wasn't because I was never religious enough. I was feature editor of the yearbook, but they kept me from being editor. It still annoys me.

"Then, in my senior year, I told the priests I wanted to apply to Harvard. They said I couldn't. They said they wouldn't forward my records or give me recommendations. They only wanted me to go to a Catholic school like Boston College. I went up to Boston on my own, and explained it to the admissions people at Harvard. No one else in my school had ever gone there. No one else in my family had completed *high school*, much less *college*, much less *Harvard*. After me, my next-younger brother went to Yale. They wouldn't forward his records, either.

"Just a few years ago, I saw a newspaper from that high school, boasting that one of their students had just gotten into Harvard. They called him the first. Times have changed there, but that boy wasn't the first.

"The second year at Harvard, my roommate started psychoanalysis. Now he's a psychiatrist. He became so terribly moody and upset that year. I never want to do that. I saw right then what too much introspection can do to you. It's a time-consuming practice. Everyone needs their armor. All I can say is this: I had a sense that doing well was showing them. It made me independent. You don't have to rely on people."

I think of today's emergency surgery, of his reliance on Culver, and guess that he's found an ally in spite of himself.

———————————

Having once decided to be a surgeon, Stearne plunged into his training with a vengeance. After graduating from Harvard college and medical school, he studied with surgeons in New York City, and, later, in London.

He had known even before he went up to Harvard that he wished to be a doctor. He is not forthcoming about his memories of medical school—a trait that turns out to be common to the profession. The experience is a long tunnel of drudgery, marked chiefly by the first bout with a cadaver, and by one's eventual emergence, transformed and professionalized—and a stranger to the innocent who started the journey four years before.

7

"You Can Do Anything
to Her and She Doesn't Move"

Stearne's mother, to my astonishment and gratitude, suggests that she save me hours of driving by meeting me for a talk halfway. I'm probably so busy, she says, and she has some hours to spare, and children nearby she wants to visit.

As fall dampens into winter, I find myself sitting with Mrs. Stearne in a sandwich shop near the water in the seacoast town where I grew up, drinking coffee from a styrofoam cup and listening to her tales of her eldest child. She is a sturdy and vivacious woman with bright blond hair, now only in her early sixties. She gave birth to Russell while still a teenager, after just a year of marriage. She remembers her son's surgical education very well, especially his year of residency, because that was in New York City, nearby, and he stopped by one day—but that comes later, doesn't it, and don't I want to know about Russell's childhood?

She speaks of his early brilliance, his good grades, his dutifulness as altar boy, his compulsiveness: "Even when he was little, my mother—his grandmother—would comment on how he'd straighten a picture if it was hanging crooked, or would walk across the floor to pick up a thread." She speaks of his solitariness, his independence, and his mischievousness in setting people up to look foolish: "His brother Lenny had to get up in the darkness to go to school one year because they were on split sessions, and it was winter, so the sun came up late. Russell woke Lenny at ten at night and told him it was six in the morning—he was late for school. Lenny dressed, and grabbed his schoolbag. He came walking down through the living room, the way he would every morning, carrying that bag. Suddenly, he got this bewildered look on his face because there were me and his father reading the paper, the way he knew we did at night, just before bedtime. It was very funny, actually."

Russell Stearne, surgeon-to-be, was the eldest. He was close to some of his brothers. When he was in his surgical residency, his mother got pregnant once more. He must have been submerged in his professional role already, judging from his mother's report of his reaction to her news. "I have seven children now. Russell is in his forties, and he has a nineteen-year-old sister. She likes him and she goes to visit them. She's about two years older than Russell's eldest child. When I became pregnant with her, Russell was nearby, working at a hospital in Manhattan. He came out to see me, and I told him I was expecting again. He surprised me so much. He got very angry. He said a woman in her early forties shouldn't have any more children. He told me, "Don't go to the hospital to have this baby and expect to come home with a live infant, because too many things can happen." He had brought along one of his obstetrics textbooks, and he pulled it out and showed me pictures—pictures of monsters, deformed babies with two heads. I was upset. I told him, 'You're lucky you're not my doctor. And it's good you're not going to be a gynecologist, talking to women the way you are talking to me!' My baby was fine."

When Stearne trained, about 5 percent of medical students were female—it's above 25 percent now. Few took up surgery; at conferences, Stearne has met "one or two" female general surgeons, but doesn't know any well. The American College of Surgeons' *Socio-Economic Factbook for Surgery 1980* says 4,200 of the nation's 102,414 surgeons are women. Stearne joined a masculine crowd in a sheltered camp, where his earnestness transformed into membership in the profession, and human suffering became evidence of the world's need for his developing craft.

Stearne has spent almost no time at large in any world in which his training and work did not supply his sense of identity, almost no time in the world of two equal sexes. His few tales of friendships with women, before his entering the shelter of his trade and his marriage, have a private glitter to them.

"When I was doing my surgical residency—the year in London, this was—there was a little black nurse from the West Indies at the hospital. She used to take off her shoe under the operating table, and she'd squeeze her toes right into the side of my shoe while I was operating. She was something. In New York, too, I had a very good time as an intern. I liked some of the nurses there. At a teaching hospital, young women come looking for fun and adventure. One of my greatest disappointments coming up here to New England is that all the nurses are country bumpkins or else Polish mamas. Still, it's always nice in the operating room. Almost all women look good with a surgical mask on. It makes the eyes beautiful."

Stearne met his future wife while both worked at a dog laboratory in Boston where a venerable patriarch of modern surgery carried out experiments. She was a lab assistant, thinking of a career as a veterinarian; he was still thinking about a career in academic medicine. Raised in alliance with a few brothers, but distant from father and mother, Stearne fell in love not only with his wife-to-be but with her family. "It's a large family and all involved with each other all the time—with reunions, big picnics, phone calls back and forth. I wanted to be part of it." She was from one of the leading families of the northern tier of Yankeedom, with banks, quarries, government officials; and his future father-in-law—whom Stearne actually does call "the grand old man"—was in charge of the whole thing. With Stearne's marriage came the celebrity due the son-in-law and surgeon-to-be as the new arrival at, his new family's special, predictable, and warm holiday celebrations, and large, ceremonial dinners. The new Mrs. Stearne gave up the dog lab. She also had aspired to being a wife and mother. She raised children, worked avidly for local charities, and swam long enough and hard enough so that, past forty, she has placed well in national competitions. "I'm busy all the time," she has said, "but I stay away from the hospital. My husband doesn't want me anywhere near there. Other doctors' wives volunteer. But he won't let me do it."

The hospital where Stearne practices surgery, like most hospitals in America, has among its chief organizational imperatives a mandate to carry out the autonomous judgments of its doctors, and to stay out of financial trouble. Stearne is helped in his work by a large staff—mostly female—whose hierarchical positions are set forth by edict and custom with nearly feudal refinement. He is invariably treated with polite deference by everyone from head nurse to cleaning woman. The small surgical staff of his hospital performed 4,090 surgical procedures in 1981, more than half of them major. If they follow the national pattern, then about two-thirds of the surgical operations done in the hospital were done on women—the national figures show that of 21 million operations performed back in 1978, about 13 million of them were done on women and 8 million on men. Men come in a quarter again as often as women because of accidents, poisonings, and violence, and have 25 percent more heart trouble, ulcers, appendicitis, hernias, head injuries, lacerations, and open wounds. Both sexes get the same amount of cancer.

Women have more hospital stays for which the finding is "benign neoplasms," or "examinations without sickness or tests with negative findings." Women have about 120 operations per thousand persons, men only 78. The most common surgery done in hospitals is gynecological—nearly four million procedures in 1978. Frequency of gynecological surgery seems to be rising. Rates of diagnostic dilation and curettage, and of hysterectomy, have gone up about 30 percent in the last ten years; the rate of Caesarean sections has recently doubled (with much attendant publicity). Five gynecological procedures—d & c, hysterectomy, tubal ligation, Caesarean, and oophorectomy—account for 30 percent of all surgery done in 1978, while in 1971 they comprised, at most, 15 percent of all surgery. The nation's general surgeons receive forty million office visits a year, and 60 percent of them are made by women.

The American College of Surgeons' 1980 factbook says there are 866 female general surgeons, and 32,000 male general surgeons. The highest percentage of female surgeons—about 10 percent—accounts for about 2,500 of the country's 25,000 obstetrician-gynecologists. Curiously, to follow the inverse case, the number of female urological surgeons—presumably operating on males—in the whole United States seems to be 26, as compared to over 7,000 male urologists.

The preponderance of male surgeons helps shape Stearne's world, but the issue is alien to him; he does not think much about it. Things do appear to be changing. About 30 percent of medical school admissions are women, and this percentage about equals the percentage of female applicants. And Stearne, whose HMO and allied university infirmary practice brings him visits from younger women, admits to having "been educated some" by a few of his more forthright patients. But in his daily work at the hospital, he seems very much a dogged survivor of the 1950s. Some of the women who work with him complain, when he's not around, but he seems to construe their differences with him as good-natured fun.

"There's one very strong women's libber here," Stearne tells me one day as we walk down a hospital corridor, "and whenever I see her I say, 'You have a gorgeous, sexy body and I'd like to take you off and examine you sometime. Doesn't that offend you as a women's libber?' And she answers me, 'Not from you, it doesn't.' " It seems to me that she topped him; he tells the story as evidence of a standoff, of happy working partners getting along, same as usual, by ribbing each other.

Standing next to the scrub sinks in the surgical corridor, he says one day to a young nurse coming from an operating room where an adult male is being circumcised, "Did you get in trouble in there, Sally? I hope you didn't make it hard for them."

In the midst of a routine hernia operation, in a rushed moment, Stearne violates standard precautionary procedure and lays a used needle down near the incision on some gauze sops, rather than handing it back to a scrub nurse for counting and disposal. The nurse scolds him. He has legal responsibility for the postoperative needle count, and a lost needle is serious trouble. "Dr. Stearne, you left a needle there!" Stearne replies, "Charlene, I think you're getting senile. I think you're slipping."

During a slack moment in another procedure, a long and tedious operation far into a patient's sick belly, Stearne places an electric scalpel, blade turned out of harm's way, against a nurse's arm. He pantomimes pressing the foot pedal that activates it, and he imitates the sound it makes when on: "Bzzzzzzzz." The nurse, playing along while holding the incision open with a retractor, pantomimes a moment of agony, and says, "Arrrgggh!"

"Myrna here is the picture of stability," Stearne comments to the assembled surgical team. "You can do anything to her and she doesn't move." Stearne and Myrna both laugh. It sounds like a complaint about an unresponsive lover.

Some nurses have attended meetings advertised on their notice board as "Assertiveness Training." Stearne has asked an organizer of these gatherings, whom he encounters at the hospital, "Why do you want nurses to be more assertive?" From the way he recounts the incident, he may be baiting her, and then

103

again, he may want to know her answer.

Two student nurses, one fine-boned, doe-eyed, notably attractive, the other sturdy, coarse-skinned, and plainer, stand
timidly inside the doorway of the operating room where Stearne
helps prepare a patient for a carotid endarterectomy. The students are already masked, although no one else in the room is
yet—everyone knows the routine, and there's little point in low-
ering one's mask until the sterile draping is getting under way.

"May we come in to observe?" the fine-boned one asks,
nearly whispering.

"Not until I see who you are," says Stearne. He walks over
and lifts her mask away from her face. She averts her eyes.
Then he playfully pulls the other student's cap down, until it's
pressing into her eyes.

For the first forty-five minutes of the surgery they watch
attentively and are ignored, with no one explaining what's happening, or why. They stand on low stools behind Stearne's back.
Stearne isolates the carotid artery from the complex anatomy of
the patient's neck. He prepares clamps to close down blood flow
through it. After clamping, he has ten minutes to do his work
and restore circulation. It is one of the few surgical procedures
that routinely entail tense, concentrated minutes. A nurse clicks
a stopwatch, and reports each minute gone. "Nine," she says,
then, "Eight." Stearne slices open the artery and cleans out the
mat of plaque that narrows it. He is deft and efficient. In only
six and a half minutes he's ready to close; he has the slit partially
stitched up in another thirty seconds. "Three minutes," says the
nurse. With such surgery, the surgeon must release the clamped
artery for a moment before completing the stitching so the
strong back pressure of blood can flush out fresh clotting. If the
wound is sealed without this flushing, clots might be pushed
onward to the brain.

Stearne glances behind him, taking measure of the student
nurses. As he unclamps, he steps sideways. A fat pulse of blood

spits from the artery and loops through the air past him, like a hurled Bloody Mary. It lands with precision, spattering the prettier student nurse's bare arm and leg, and streaking across her dress. Playing with blood here is not as grave a sacrilege as it may sound at first. In surgery, blood seems of little consequence. It's like money in the middle of a poker game. One's notion of its value changes, excitingly. In fact, Stearne had done a similar thing to me the first time I had seen him performing an operation, months earlier. I thought of it then as an initiation ritual, a hazing that had touched me with blood—nasty, but counting me in. Perhaps it is that again, but the circulating nurse sees this repetition of the event in a different light.

"Here, look what he did!" she says in a comforting voice. She looks disgusted, reaches out and touches the student. She swabs the blood off the student's arm and leg with a sterile towel. Deflecting attention from the intrusion, avoiding trouble, the student says, "Oh, I don't care—it's not my dress."

"Doctors are little boys and we treat them like that," says the circulating nurse.

Meanwhile, Stearne's attention remains on the procedure. He quickly finishes the repair, and has the carotid sealed and unclamped just as the nurse calls, "One minute." He has completed a technically demanding procedure without incident. Formal report for carotid surgery: "Normal interior carotid stenosis . . . proceeding medially we identified the carotid sheath. . . . Careful sharp and blunt dissection were pursued." In the coming weeks the patient thrives. The student nurses have learned things they must know about some surgeons—if not about surgery.

————◆————

Stearne recalls another black nurse from the days of his residency in New York—one who figured out how to hold her own against him. "She greeted me effusively when I came on duty. She stuck out her hand, saying, 'Hi, Doc.' The hand was covered with feces from the bedpans she'd been cleaning out.

She thought it was very funny, and laughed." He is still astonished by her.

———————————————

A former patient of Stearne's brought suit against him a few years ago for malpractice. It's an occupational hazard—one that has raised the cost of surgery because surgeons pass along high malpractice insurance bills. Surgeons cut on the basis of probabilities. From time to time, given the complexity of the body, bureaucracy, and human nature, they're bound to be wrong. A minority of surgeons do some surgery on the basis of opportunity rather than need. And once in a while, even when they have not erred or been opportunistic, surgeons get sued. In this case, the fact of the suit, and even the fifteen minutes of his medical life that Stearne had spent with the patient, seemed usual enough, part of the normal experience of a surgeon. Nearly all surgeons get sued. They defend themselves. One moment in the subsequent legal activity did seem unusual, however.

Five years before, the patient—"Ms. Cooper"—had come on a spring Saturday morning to the emergency room, complaining that her belly hurt and had hurt for some days. The HMO she belonged to contacted Stearne and asked him to meet the patient. Stearne examined her at the hospital. He ordered urine and blood tests. And he decided that she probably suffered from gastroenteritis—a viral infection—and would very likely cure herself in a day or so. If not, she was told to call him back.

She never did call back, but two weeks later, in a hospital elsewhere, she was operated on for a massive infection of her fallopian tube and ovary—pelvic inflammatory disease or PID. Because of this infection, she became sterile. Even after surgery, the disease went on and on. Her marriage suffered and collapsed.

She felt, afterward, that the infection most probably had started before Stearne examined her, and had caused the symptoms he diagnosed as gastroenteritis. She suspected that the infection had resulted from her having in place an intrauterine device, a Dalkon shield—which had already been implicated in the medical literature for contributing to such infections.

During his physical examination of Ms. Cooper, Stearne had failed to note that she was wearing an IUD. The oversight, according to some medical sources, is understandable, because the thread extending from an IUD may wander and no other trace of the IUD may be visible or palpable. PID was coming to be a widely considered diagnosis, but its connection to IUDs had only recently been established.

Ms. Cooper sued Robins pharmaceutical company, manufacturers of the Dalkon shield. They settled out of court. She also sued Stearne and several other doctors. After a morning of surgery, and lunch in town, one late-fall day, Stearne kept an appointment at the county courthouse, to testify in a discovery hearing on the case. The participants assembled in an ornate oak courtroom—oak defendants' chairs, oak judge's bench, oak pews, oak wall panels, and a ceiling mural of Justice with cherubs. A maroon-suited attorney perhaps in her fifties, counsel for Robins, represented Stearne too. The plaintiff had sent a lawyer who looked to be fresh from law school. She had long black hair, and studied until the last moment, her fingers tugging paper after paper from a fat file she had pulled from her briefcase.

Stearne refused to be sworn in. It seemed capricious to me. He said his word would do; he said his religion—he's a more or less lapsed Catholic—prevented him from taking the oath. His testimony was accepted anyway. He sat at a table in the middle of the room. Ms. Cooper's lawyer questioned Stearne's memory, which actually continued to be quite remarkable.

"You saw the plaintiff for this examination five years ago, at about two in the afternoon. Do you remember the occasion?" the lawyer asked.

"Yes, very well."

"Can you describe her appearance?" She bobbed in toward him with every inquiry.

"She was a skinny girl. Light hair. Somewhat homely."

The lawyer's mouth clenched. She expressed herself only

by an angry shake of the head, as if to clear her mind, and by more sharply posed questions: "How tall was she?" and: "If you had detected the presence of an IUD, would you have treated the case any differently?"

"I did not detect it. And I do not treat ifs," Stearne answered this one.

"Were you familiar with Dalkon shields?"

"My wife had one."

"Do you know the symptoms of pelvic inflammatory disease?"

"Fever, rapid pulse, sweats, pain, signs of pain on pelvic examination—what we call the chandelier sign: when you move the cervix, the patient will literally jump off the table."

———————

Some months later, Stearne settled his part of the case out of court. Long afterward, he tells me, he now recognizes his lack of tact in refusing to be sworn in, in using the term "girl," and in speaking about her as "homely." He tells me he has regretted these actions.

His perverse candor in court, where it may have worked contrary to his best interests, has something to do with his line of work. He's hired for his technical skills, and not for his social values or personality. The sometimes desperate pressure that goes with patient contact—to please help out, doc—isolates him, raises his guard, tempts him to push all patients back, to ward them off by reifying them. It seems unregenerate but also unexceptional for him to wish to forget the personhood, and the vulnerability, that he shares with every patient. Patients (and staff too) often have a peculiar ambivalence—resenting doctors' high-handedness in general, but celebrating those doctors working with them in particular. Doctors feel equally ambivalent. Patients (as surgeons tell each other in the locker room) act silly, don't do what's good for them, feign illness, fail to discern manifest illness in time; they are also dear souls to be cherished and guarded, and sacrifices of one's own are to be made for them.

For both parties in this uncomfortable deal, adulation and cherishing often conceal nastier feelings. The unfairness of disease—which may triumph in spite of efforts to eradicate it—helps shape the transactions on both sides.

Medical reformers write about a more just world in which doctors are ordinary, in which none notices who's beautiful or homely, in which you can see a doctor on a few minutes' notice, in which doctors guard the workplace and the environment, working even harder to prevent than to treat disease, in which they take time to help people understand how to care for their own bodies, to watch their diets, to never smoke, and to exercise. In the meanwhile, we seem to need sworn enemies of death. They will disappoint us, sooner or later, in every case, but we have allowed them to take on power and privilege, and prejudice, in return, perhaps, for both their practical and their ceremonial chores.

———————

It's late evening in the pediatric ward. Sick kids lie four to a room, nestled down in blue cotton. They are so little. Contained in brown-barred cribs, they seem like small mammals asleep in their wing of a zoo. But above peeling decals of elves and pale flowers on the cribs' headboards, intravenous medications drip through thin tubing into children's arms. The dominant sound in the corridor is the quiet hiss of labored wheezing, layered with a hearty melody line of soprano snoring, from the far end of the hall. Behind a nearly closed bedroom door, two parents murmur in tired conversation. One breaks into laughter.

Stearne stops at the nurses' station, finds a chart, and walks slowly back to a private room. He wants to see his patient—an eleven-year-old girl—once more before her surgery tomorrow. She's sitting up in bed and reading a fashion magazine. A mature eleven. The pale skin of her thin face seems flushed, in the shadow of a profusion of long black hair. She has the sickly, desolate beauty once expected of languishing tuberculars. Her expression, when she looks at Stearne, is tired and blank. She wears a little girl's white flannel nightgown. Horses gallop all over it.

"You set for tomorrow?" asks Stearne quietly.

"I guess so."

"Was your mom here?"

"Yeah, but she had to go take care of the other kids."

"Does it still hurt?"

She becomes more animate. "Yeah. Before, about an hour ago, it hurt real bad—over here," she says, pointing to her upper belly. Stearne presses down hard on the spot with his fingertips, then lets up quickly. She tenses, but only slightly.

"You'll do fine," he says as we walk out.

"What she's got is something unusual, but it's on the books, and I'm going to take care of it. Chronic appendicitis. It's described." In his dictation of the record of her symptoms, available to the hospital review committee that looks into cases in which normal tissue is removed during surgery, he takes the unusual step of citing from one of the annals of surgery the specific reference to chronic appendicitis that lends strength to his diagnosis.

"Will it come out all red and infected looking?" I ask. I have seen him do a routine operation for acute appendicitis quickly and deftly, just a few weeks earlier. The offending little cul-de-sac of gut had come out purple, swollen, and ugly.

"It might not. About one in ten patients with an *acute* abdomen—and all the other symptoms of *acute* appendicitis—turns out not to have it. The tissue review committee glances at all cases in which tissue is removed that pathology says is normal. If you run about one normal case for each nine with pathology, they don't bother you. But that's why I put that citation in my report. I believe that's what she's got. She's missed a lot of school over the past few years, complaining about this sort of abdominal pain. She was in the hospital for a GI workup—and it was normal. But she may have impacted feces there. And the operation may stop her having symptoms whether they're real or not."

"Do you know anything about her family life?"

110

"I don't know much about it."

It's a touchy area. The way medical protocols are set up, the examining physician may judge to the best of his ability that a patient's symptoms add up to "chronic appendicitis," and may then take action on the diagnosis. This diagnosis, however, is difficult to corroborate by pathology. If offered only occasionally, it will get by the inquiry of a tissue review committee because normal findings are no surprise. Some medical authorities have indeed recognized such a disease. Some surgeons have told me it offers them an opportunity they feel they need, to deal with some sorts of obscure but chronic abdominal pain.

However, Dr. Roy Barnett, a professor of clinical pathology at Yale and author of a leading pathology textbook, has told me that in his opinion, "Chronic appendicitis is a nonsensical diagnosis, one that only the older physicians—the GPs who still do appendectomies—might use now, but that does more to protect the surgeon than to predict what will be found."

A few days after the surgery, Stearne mentioned to me that the eleven-year-old's postoperative pathology work had indeed shown a normal appendix. "She'll never get appendicitis now," he said, "and besides that, I probably cured her symptoms of abdominal pain. She feels I took out what was wrong."

8

"Doctors Are the Technicians, Not the Caregivers"

Stearne does about a dozen mastectomies annually. In the past year or so, he has joined with the growing minority of surgeons who look with favor upon lumpectomies and partial breast removals followed by radiation as proper treatment for selected cases of breast cancer. In 1977, he did not do lumpectomies—few surgeons took them seriously. He performed a "modified Halsted"—a radical mastectomy—upon a young psychologist, Mimi White, who had come to him with a thumb-sized lump of cancer growing in her right breast. As Mimi White's account of her surgery reveals, Stearne's antics with nurses and his courtroom misjudgment occlude a kinder side of him. Few operations stir questions of sexual identity more profoundly than mastectomy, as Mimi White came to realize.

"I didn't think of lumpectomies, either," she says. We chat in a restaurant not far from her office. In her late thirties now, she carries herself with grace. Her gestures are full, enthusiastic motions and she laughs easily even as she remembers her experience. "I blame myself—I think appropriately—for not doing so, and for not getting second opinions from Boston, where such new thought is liable to be tried out first.

"I'm an anesthesiologist's daughter. I had no illusions about surgeons. I wanted a good technician, and Dr. Stearne came recommended to my father and to me as the best in town, which I still think is true. My dad used to call surgeons the 'flight boys'—technicians who didn't have to know a lot. I was prepared for that. I had a nice internist who was knowledgeable, and sympathetic enough for my needs.

"I used to have a horror of even imagining the blood flowing through my body. I'd lie in my husband's arms, and if I'd feel his blood coursing I'd have to move. The skin hides things. He found the lump in my breast—top of the right one—while we were making love. He told me the next morning, not that night. I felt it, and as soon as I felt it I knew it was serious. The internist felt it, and sent me right to Dr. Stearne. I saw him about five days after I'd first felt it.

"He was a classic. He looked like he'd just taken a shower after playing tennis—self-satisfied, so clean, a little flab from too many steaks. I felt all along with him that he wanted to be the one in charge. I also felt that a feminist had laced into him before I arrived on the scene, had pinned his ears back and said, 'All right, here's the things a woman needs who comes in with a lump in her breast.'

"I thought that here's a man so skilled he's *trying*—he doesn't want to appear clumsy or brutal. I never felt he shared my fear, or grief, or pain. I can't imagine him having that. But I knew about surgeons. I knew *why* he couldn't. In fact, I was grateful to that imaginary feminist who must have gone at him. He took it step by step—wouldn't let my scared questions get in his way, or take things too fast. It was, 'First we'll see if this is so, and then if it is, we'll see if this is so, and then, even if it is cancer, we'll do this and this and this.' " Mimi White pauses and sips her coffee. She is plainly reluctant to stir up matters she has allowed to settle. She stretches her arms, then goes on.

"The X-rays were a horrible experience. The technicians were lovely, but they have to treat the breasts like meat—pick them up, turn them to fit under the machine. There's never any reading material in X-ray—I read the labels on the machines.

The radiologist came in to help the technician. I wonder if doctors know how much their slightest gesture is interpreted by anxious patients.

"Then Dr. Stearne told me the results, and that's the point where things could have been better. He said let's operate, but there's a ninety-six percent chance it's benign. Later, he admitted that if he'd thought, in advance, that it would have been the particular type of cancer it was—an unusual and slow-growing one—he'd have given me some odds that would have prepared me better for what happened.

"I'd always thought that if it were a case of a breast or my life, I'd have no trouble saying, 'Breast it is'—saying that breasts' importance is just some *Playboy* fetish. That reaction was a 'trust medicine,' doctor's-daughter reaction. Lumpectomies had been done and studied a little bit already, and for what I had, would have done just as well. I didn't know that then, which is why I didn't even consider getting a second opinion.

"The breast does matter. No amount of liberal cant will assure you afterwards you're not scarred; you see a cripple, and you're repelled somewhere down deep, do-gooder or not. You can't imagine what it feels like to put on your prosthesis. It becomes habit, but never fails to make me think that I'm not whole. Of course, the issue of possibly still having cancer—I've been symptom-free for years—ties in with my emotional attitudes.

"Dr. Stearne told me the next steps, about having the operation and about taking the lymph nodes. He avoided elaborate descriptions. I was grateful. I was upset, but didn't feel toward him any worship or sexual transference, as I had to some doctors earlier in life. I was aware of my feelings in a detached, clinical way. I looked for this because of my father's being a doctor and because I'm so psychologically oriented.

"Going into the hospital is strange. You go in and you're not sick. But you get into your nightgown and get into bed. My new roommates' problems instantly became important to me. On one side, a salt-of-the-earth type with a bowel obstruction.

Her doctor sleazed in and out in a white tie and black shirt. He hardly related to her. I thought she should get a real doctor. A young professional woman next to me on the other side was cold, but nice.

"Dr. Stearne came in briefly, bustling, but he seemed superfluous on the wards. The nurses were the heart and soul of the care, and they were wonderful. Doctors are the technicians, not the caregivers. They think they're kings, but they're not—that's the secret joke of life on the hospital floors.

"I went down to the OR later than scheduled—eleven or so, which was annoying because you have to lie around, feeling well, but without breakfast, worrying. They said on the floor that Stearne goes very fast. I didn't know if I'd wake up missing a breast or not, and that's bad, because with two possibilities, you can't concentrate on what you need to think about in order to adjust. You're hung, suspended. I thought about the previous evening, when I hugged my daughter in my hospital room—she was only four then—and said, 'Goodbye.'

"They grogged me up—shot and pills. It was like a release. I started to cry. The tears poured out of my eyes. It was the basic human terror of surgery: I was afraid of dying. I felt helpless going down the corridor; I can still remember the faces going by, that I looked up at as they were wheeling me.

"A magical thing happened. The orderly who wheeled me—he was a man in his fifties, and so tender. He looked at me, and he said, half to himself, 'She's crying.' We went out of an elevator. The next thing I hear him say is, 'You got me so upset I got you off on the wrong floor.' We got back into the elevator, and down into the surgical suite, and into a room with other patients, waiting, and he parked me. He leaned over then, and said, 'You know it's O.K. to cry; it's human.' I'm not a believer, but under the drugs, I felt like God had sent me an angel down there when I was in hell. I was so grateful.

"I saw green. I saw bright lights. I saw Stearne, but I didn't recognize him at first behind his mask. The anesthesiologist or someone was trying to put a needle into the back of my hand and kept missing. Dr. Stearne was very nice. I remember that he

115

said to everyone, 'You be careful with her, she's special. Treat her well.' That's the last thing I remember.

"I've got no memory of the recovery room, or the trip back up to my room late that night. I remember being put back on the bed, and then my husband leaning over me, saying, 'It was cancer.' I moaned. I said, 'Oh, no.' Later, he told me that that cut him to the core, but it was right to say it immediately. He didn't want me to be in suspense. He sat next to my bed and read and held my hand all night. Whenever I woke up I had questions. He had had a long talk with Dr. Stearne. He said later that Dr. Stearne had been very understanding and complete in answering. That gave my husband answers to the questions I kept asking.

"The next three days were the worst part. Dr. Stearne had taken out my lymph nodes on the right side, and the lab report telling whether the cancer had spread into them wouldn't come back until Friday. I can't explain the intensity of the agony of waiting. The nurses did what they could. They found a nurse from another floor who had had a mastectomy herself. This woman was tough, but very sympathetic. She sat down on the bed and talked to me. She drew the curtain around the bed as she told her story, then undid her uniform and showed me the scar. She slipped out the prosthesis and let me hold it. It was warm from her. I felt sorry for her, and also thankful she showed me the equipment. She obviously was a very good nurse in the best sense—she combined realism and optimism. Still, the basic experience then, for me, was fear.

"Dr. Stearne had arranged some complicated plan where he would come to my hospital room Friday, in late morning, with the news, after my husband would have put the kids in school and driven down. Friday morning I lay there. I knew he was in the hospital already, because I heard him being paged, and I knew he knew the results. Then he appeared, within moments. Seeing him, before my husband arrived, I knew he had good news, or else he would have waited. 'It's all fine. The results are in,' he said to me.

"I just started to cry. He sat down and after a minute he

said, 'Why don't you call your husband now?' I did, and on the phone my husband started to cry too. Dr. Stearne never quite broke out of his role, but I think he was moved, even though he showed no personal reaction. Later on, the nurses celebrated with me. They were more able to blur their personal and professional worlds. I felt much better. I thought I had a chance.

"While I was getting stronger, the nurses were so kind. They came in and asked about my lab reports. One put a garbage bag over me with a hole in it for my head, and washed my hair. They sat and talked with me. I could see they identified with me more than with most other patients. It's funny, but I soon got so I didn't want to go home.

"My mother was very upset. At that time she was having some hard times of her own, and my trouble made hers harder. I discovered something about having cancer. I felt I had to help her deal with it. Later, I had to help a lot of people deal with it. Having cancer had something to do—not directly—with the fact that my husband and I split up. I came out of the experience feeling you can't separate the body and the self. I am an attractive woman without a breast. I developed a fierce will to get better, to get my strength back. I played volleyball a month after the operation. It was agony to raise my arm and hit the ball.

"I started going out with the man I now live with. The first time he saw my scar, he burst out crying. Sometimes it gets in the way of his being attracted to me. He's honest about it, and I'm grateful—it goes very deep. He gives expression to how I feel about myself. To have someone else in on that struggle with accepting something that you don't want, that can't change, and that does matter, is powerful. It makes us close. But I hate it. When I'm mad, I say, 'Wait until someone saws off your buttock.' That's the closest analogy for a man—a buttock is sexy and prominent, but not the main event.

"I resumed my life, and I learned a lot. I say one job of a maimed person, or a cripple, is to help the people around to be comfortable. I notice acquaintances studying my breasts, perhaps trying to tell which one is missing, or if they can see the line of the edge of the prosthesis. They look away when I notice. But they shouldn't feel guilty for natural curiosity. I have a neighbor, a paraplegic, who fell off a tree he was working on. He says he wants people to ignore his wheelchair, to treat him just like a person with full use of his body. But that's impossible, and it just creates strained relationships, because it forces the other person to cover up, and things don't get discussed.

"I went back for many examinations with Dr. Stearne. The first time after the bandage was off, he asked if the scar bothered me. I told him I hadn't brought myself to look. He pushed my head down to look at it. That was O.K. of him to do. I'm actually grateful. And a long time afterwards, he apologized, he actually volunteered an apology. He said he hadn't thought it might be this unusual, slow-growing tumor it turned out to be, or he wouldn't have quoted me such reassuring odds that it was benign, before the operation.

"I think that if he failed in any way, it was in not considering the alternatives enough—that this type of tumor may have been a candidate for lumpectomy. I also have the overall impression that he is very guarded against the pain of a woman losing her breast. He wasn't mean. He wasn't sexist. He is an arrogant *doctor*, and it comes across. But he was also considerate and thoughtful as a doctor. As I've said, I was as responsible—or more—for not getting another opinion.

"Years later—it's been over six years free of cancer now—I got curious about lumpectomies, thinking what would happen if I ever needed another operation. Also, just putting to rest what happened to me. So I made an appointment with a wonderful man—very old, and long retired now, named Dr. Oliver Cope, who pioneered lumpectomy work in Boston. Dr. Stearne must have gotten scared that I was going to sue him. He made it very hard for me to get my records. I finally had to go through relatives who work in the hospital. I was mad at him for a little while, but that incident doesn't change my overall impression: that he was a very good surgeon, and that he went to great pains to treat me as well as he was able to do—given his limitations, and with the exception of that records business."

9

"These Girls Don't Pinch Any Organs"

Danny Andersson is a milder sort than Stearne, more genial and less likely to engage in any but the most casual and directed conversation with nurses or patients. He regularly calls nurses "babe," with democratic disregard for their ages. He reassures a family doctor who telephones to refer a nervous patient to him, "Don't worry, Louie, I'm used to handling scared elderly gals." In surgery he comments that a patient who has been operated on before "has more scar tissue than a millipede's got tits."

His attitudes are subdued, have little effect on his work, and rarely ruffle even those who notice them. He seems an apt emblem for surgeons in this respect—doing what is done generally, in a profession where what is done generally reflects the attitudes that prevail outside medicine too. Doctors may heal disease, but they seem to feel little more of a mandate to heal society in general than do the practitioners of any other trade. In this respect, they may especially disappoint those who idealize them. Andersson tells a frequent patient, a diabetic black man whose hair is turning gray, "You're finally seeing the light, Bill—you're getting white." He remarks, about a nationally famous actor he once examined, "I'm one of the few people to have gotten to have a finger up that fellow's ass." He has been known to call fat persons "blimp," and mentally retarded persons "idiot"—neither to their faces. The setting of surgery, for all its sterility, plays out the inevitabilities of the real world again and again.

———————————

Blood flow is concentrically laminar. Like the runoff from last night's storm, which still trickles through the street gutters outside, Andersson's patient's blood fans around obstructions, eddies and slows at crimps and corners, and there dumps its rubble. The long, lanky man sleeping lightly in the stretcher outside the OR door, awaiting the surgeon's arrival from an early-morning emergency operation elsewhere, has badly clogged arteries. Arteries don't clog uniformly. Plaque clumps at the intersections—where the aorta bifurcates into iliacs that lead into the thighs, then where the femoral arteries fork into the popliteals, shunting blood to the lower legs.

In genetically fortunate persons, circulatory flotsam-cleaning apparatus remains intact into old age, and little plaque forms. My mother's father died in his fifties, of circulatory compromise. His aorta burst, no doubt years after plaque had decreased its elasticity and strength, and an aneurysm slowly swelled its degrading walls into a bulge—opaque, then sheer, then torn. I take this work personally.

Danny Andersson has driven back to his home hospital, on schedule, squinting into the morning sun along streets icy from the fall storm. He carries his radio into the operating room in a plastic bag. He's relieved to be on time, he says to a nurse, and he's already done a pacemaker at the other hospital. Scheduling offers surgeons an arena for their sharp political scuffling. Andersson compromises, gracefully, where he must, and claims to like the results. Once bounced from the schedule for lateness, a surgeon may not get more OR time for hours. "I like operating in the morning best," Andersson says, tying on a cotton hat for the second time this morning.

Andersson checks the selection of thin white arterial grafts a nurse has laid out in the busy operating room. In the early

1950s, a company making urinary catheters set out to design prosthetic blood vessels. Some of the earliest were knitted on a machine for manufacturing shoelaces, by a circle of tiny needles. Although a few early grafts tended to dissolve eventually, the new models, of Dacron and Teflon and a plastic fabric called Gore-Tex, stand up to eternity. Grafts are frequently corrugated to withstand crushing as the body twists and tightens around them. They occasionally become infected—a serious complication—but don't erode nowadays.

The man anesthetized on the table has been here before. His body is welted with surgical scars, and with the wales of arterial prostheses already in place. He's in his fifties; he's had one leg replumbed, and has an artificial aorta. The other leg has acted up. Yet, Andersson says somewhat proudly, the patient has been working in a factory again until recently, although he hasn't treated himself carefully. He still smokes. He eats incautiously. His scarred paunch sags to the right as this otherwise thin man, still dozing, receives the rites of prophylaxis. Andersson paints the man's bottom orange, then moves up to paint the belly, and down to paint the legs. Doreen, the devoted assistant, slips sterile leggings onto the swabbed legs. Each bootie has a transparent cellophane window over the top of the foot. "We make them up to Dr. Andersson's design," says Doreen. He can check circulation to the feet as he works.

"They're a nifty little number," says Andersson. "After you hook up the new plumbing, if you've done it right—and you better—the cellophane windows steam up, like a bathroom mirror. You can tell if you did O.K."

A fourth-year surgical resident—a tall, dark, and handsome one who is a favorite of Andersson's, one he's said "will go on to be a fine surgeon"—irritates Andersson now. He's absent. He should be scrubbed in and helping with the preparation. Today's circulating nurse, who seems particularly young and wears a flowered scrub cap that is not part of the standard regalia, tries to smooth matters for the missing doctor. She has gray eyes with lovely smile lines, wears a dress that is notably short—more miniskirt than work smock, and she says, "It's 'cause he had to

121

go up to the emergency room, Dr. Andersson. He'll be right back."

Andersson ignores the information, and abruptly begins the operation alone, cutting into the lower abdomen as if he's a tailor turning to the next piece of a large batch of work. The staff arranges itself—anesthesiologist to the head of the table, nurses soon to their retractors, Doreen to Andersson's right hand, watching carefully over her tool tables and infallibly handing on the right item wordlessly. The beginnings of all operations upon the abdomen are the same. Layers of skin and fat must be parted, slowly. Bleeding must be stifled. This beginning is routine. As the incision develops and the flasks of saline and medication slowly drip into the unconscious man on the table, the circulating nurse goes about her chores, dancing elaborately the whole time. She bends and splits apart a sealed package so Doreen can draw out sterile needles. As she offers the needles, she's doing a box step, and kicking to the side, now and then, and all the while she hums a jaunty tune. "Mmmmmmmmm."

Her name is Chloe, and I identify her as the subject of surgeons' locker room gossip. Her especially upstanding breasts have been mentioned, a few days before, as having perhaps been "enlarged" by a surgeon. She is, at the moment, playful and far more lively than her colleagues. She seems distracted, of two worlds.

"Hard night! What a night!" she exclaims. She hums on. The older nurses smile. Andersson looks up, amused. They've seen her play this part before. "Again, this morning!" she says, looking full of new love. She casts her eyes down, studies the sick, cut man on the table. Perhaps at this moment she remembers, actually thinks of the wonder of a hearty life—and that's an emotional, and therefore risky, act in this room where feelings are so often secrets hidden even from self-discovery.

"I don't want to die on *my* back!" she blurts out. The patient is wide open. Andersson ties off small vessels, severs muscle, has now cleared the way further in. Routine. Everyone looks over at Chloe, taking in what she's said. She laughs a high, musical laugh. She defends her assertion. "I *don't* want to die on my back."

Andersson asks Doreen for a clamp. He does say, "Babe," and also, "Thanks."

Across the room from the patient, another stranger has been installed, a nameless student nurse in striped uniform who watches Chloe and the operation while turned sideways to the action, her hands both pressed down upon a stack of folded linen. From her corner she stares over her right shoulder at the crowd around the operating table. She stays that way, as if she's a deactivated robot. This posture, taken up during preparation of the patient, was suggested to her by a senior nurse who had escorted her in and installed her there. It does keep her clear of sterile areas, although she might have been shown—as I was the first time I entered surgery—what few areas are sacrosanct. It is an instructive posture. As she learns, by observing, how to serve well (and, perhaps, how to dance), she learns, from her own enforced stance, of the institution's careless distrust of her, of the ritualized positions it's designed for her.

"*Not* on my *back*," says Chloe again. This time the laughter in the room sounds raucous. The comment has lost its sting third time out. She's converted it to something more familiar here, affirming a raunchy liveliness in the face of the patient's hard luck.

Andersson is getting down to where he has unroutine decisions to make and business to do. He repositions the nurses holding the spreaders and addresses himself to the question of their function here. "Could they be replaced by a self-retaining retractor? Yes, they could. But it wouldn't be as good for the patient. These girls don't pinch any organs. And they can shift around the moment I tell them to, like just now. But you can notice which one sleeps on the job. . . . "

Chloe takes up the challenge. "You haven't been working much after four P.M., have you, Doctor? If I take my vacation a different time from you, I can go . . . let's see . . . three months on my usual shift without doing any vascular surgery with you," she says.

"She's complaining because she had to come back in to help me with a case at nine at night a few days ago," Andersson says.

"Flattery will get you everywhere," sings Chloe.

The tall surgical resident rushes in, finally, and Chloe peels open a pack of rubber gloves and slips them around his hands. The nurses on retractor duty shift position to the left to accommodate him. "Sorry. Broken arm in the ER," he explains to Andersson. He has to lean down in order to work.

"I did a reduction in the ER the other night without anesthesia," Andersson says, continuing to cut. "The guy was absolutely soused."

The anesthesiologist, silent until now, commences idle chat, about his recent vacation in the Arizona desert. "The wife wanted to pick up some of that Mexican turquoise jewelry."

The operation is a variation on a theme that's grown familiar to me. Andersson has made four openings in the patient. One pair, into each thigh, reaches down through thigh muscle to plaque deposits at the bifurcations of femoral and popliteal arteries. The other pair, in the lower abdomen, exposes the femoral arteries' upper connections, to the iliacs. The function of this surgery is to sew in Dacron tubes, on both sides, that will bridge the distance between slits, bypassing blockage.

"Let's bring out the tunnel," Andersson says to Doreen. She hands him a very imposing device, a ramrod within a tube, the rod fitting tightly within its sleeve, extending through it, and ending in a solid bullet tip. Andersson accepts the foot-long assembly and shoves it quite slowly and deliberately along, under the skin, through the half foot of belly fat between the incisions. Its tip creeps along under the skin, a mouse under an orange quilt, and emerges right in front of the resident, who grabs onto it.

"We're going fem-fem," Andersson announces resolutely. He has been feeling the patient's poor vessels, making a survey of plumbing sites, and in view of the man's previous surgery, has chosen this slightly unusual cross-connection rather than the more typical direct femoral-popliteal bypass. The two gentlemen handle the tunnel, and their conversation wanders to a new restaurant in town.

"You don't choose the menu," Andersson explains. "They give you whatever they want. Couple of fags, but great food. Then in the men's john I see a red rose-covered toilet seat and a stall shower. On the floor was soap. Here are these guys playing drop-the-soap—but great food."

"Bend over!" says the resident, imagining the shower scene. What might the drugged patient be dreaming now?

The resident ties a heavy black thread to the bullet tip. Power lines get strung across canyons and huge ships get moored by this method. A light line is paid out, and used to haul heavier cable across. The thread tunneled across the patient's abdomen will lead the new Dacron femoral artery from its connection with a clear blood source on the right side, over to the left leg. Then another section will be tunneled down the right leg. Andersson draws the inner rod, thread attached, back through the tunnel. The resident secures the end of the replacement artery to the thread. Andersson draws the graft through both tunnel and the belly toward himself, by pulling on the thread. When it's through, he slips the tunnel out around it, leaving the graft in place. "The black stripe running down the length of the graft's to help make sure you don't twist the thing while you're putting it in," he says. "An idiot stripe. If you need it, you shouldn't be doing the job."

He probes about for a while, then points into the wound in front of the resident. "You know what you're seeing there?" he asks.

"An anomalous branch below the anterior femoral artery?"

"You're smart for a resident. If I show you too much, you'll end up putting me out of business."

What the hands do proceeds independently of the surgeon's talk. They sew graft ends onto clamped, slit vessels, giving form and sense to the damage they've done. There's technique to it, and style. Andersson cuts his graft end on the diagonal, to make a long cross section of a joint. It will crimp less and take more stitches than if the graft were lopped off square and then sewed into the artery. Each stitch will bear less pressure, and the oval shape will force the opening to stay wide. Andersson's stitches

125

come out fine, close, uniformly tight.

Across the patient's body, the resident sews another graft end. Experience does count. Andersson finishes his stitchery in half the time the resident is taking. Andersson notices the younger surgeon momentarily tangled in his own elbows, wrists, and thread, as he rounds back after sewing half the circle. Andersson reaches over the table, sews, returns the thread and needle to the resident only when things are straightened out.

Eventually, both resident and surgeon unclamp. And the resident's wound fills with blood. He clamps off the artery again and sucks the wound clear. The aspirator keeps clogging with small bits of tissue that float in the wound. He inspects. "I buttonholed the artery," the resident confesses in a flat voice. Andersson has said he doesn't mind the residents making understandable errors as long as they are honest about them—he just doesn't like surprises. He's responsible. And it is not surprising that this has happened. The difference between clearing away the plaque and puncturing the wall is a millimeter's thickness of calcified, slippery vessel. The error causes inconvenience, but is not a desperate mistake. Andersson's surgery, done in a teaching hospital, always takes half again as long as Stearne's, done with another experienced surgeon across the table. "When I teach, I feel I'm passing the torch," Andersson has said.

Under Andersson's closer supervision, the resident cuts a small patch, like a Band-Aid spot, to fit, stitches it on the buttonholed artery, and unclamps. The leakage persists. Andersson comes around the table and looks at the damage carefully. "It's in a nasty place. You got a hell of a hole in there. That whole back wall is frayed," he says. He joins in the sewing. He's humming now himself, enjoying this moment of improvisation.

When he unclamps, finally, ooze, but no plash of blood, signals that the operation is nearly over. "On femoral endarterectomies," Andersson confesses as the two men watch the new graft pulse strongly, "there's an easy side and a hard side. One side's done forehand, and one backhand. I gave you the hard side."

"Nice backflow," says the resident. They wait another few

minutes before closing, to see if trouble will develop. A few surgeons I've observed seem to proceed blithely amidst chaos. Andersson turns mess into organization, wound into treatment. His every measured step straightens up chaos. Part of his craft is the consistency of his detailed foresight; like a good carpenter, he does small things that make steps an hour down the line easier.

Andersson points as condensation quickly forms inside the windows atop the patient's sterile booties. The gray feet redden. "The result of increased vascularity," Andersson announces. The work of saints turns out to be done by mere mortals with good backup procedures.

Andersson plucks sops of gauze from the wound and flips them, one by one, half the width of the operating room with his tweezers, and he never misses the collection pail.

"My aim improves every day," he says.

Chloe, her work concluding, watches this show. She groans at his mock conceit.

"Like my personality?" Andersson asks.

"Maybe."

"You know where the next sponge is going?" Andersson waves the long tweezers at her. Everyone laughs. The resident stitches the patient closed.

———————————◆———————————

The surgeons' dressing room, where we change, and where Andersson then calls the patient's wife, has gotten busy. Younger surgeons come in, joking, dress quickly in operating greens, and move out to work. The chief of surgery sits in the corner, under a portrait of the founder of the hospital, glowering and reading the *Atlantic Monthly*. With everyone dressed in green, there's a deceptive appearance of democracy here that seems to extend from professors of surgery down to male operating room technicians who, like Doreen, have only a year of training in this special job.

"The real star of my surgery is Doreen," Andersson says

confidingly to me as we leave. She awaits us in the hall, now wearing a white uniform.

"If I fell down faint in the middle of an operation, she could finish up. She wouldn't, of course. Another surgeon would. But when things are happening fast, she's the one in charge of the OR in actuality. If someone starts to do something she's not happy with, and I don't notice because I'm concentrating on my part of things, she'll say something. If she doesn't get anywhere, she'll let me know too." Doreen beams at this public accolade.

Doreen and I have something in common: Our liberty in the hospital depends on our proximity to Andersson. She's paid by him; I'm invited along by him. The few occasions when I've found myself alone in the surgeons' locker room while Andersson darts off to do business elsewhere are the only times I've been asked to account for my presence; strays became someone else's worry, and whoever noticed me acted accordingly. I've watched Doreen at similar times. Occasionally, nurses who are used to running the operating room during other surgeons' work reassert their authority, suddenly ignoring Doreen's suggestions and issuing their own.

On one occasion, her independence from hospital protocol allowed her to do a favor for a nurse. A team had just completed an angiogram. The patient had to be wheeled back into intensive care, down the hall. But there was a "code blue" on in intensive care—doctors and nurses had just rushed in to try and revive a dying patient. To keep down confusion, nurses have a standing order: Never return patients to intensive care during such times. "You wheel her right in there, will you?" a nurse asks Doreen. "They can't say anything to *you*." She does. They can't, they don't, and Andersson and Doreen soon head off to lunch together.

Doreen is aware of her confused station in hospital life. "It isn't a recognized field—surgical technician. If I had to work for the hospital, the RNs and LPNs would be all over me. I'd be third man on the totem pole in the OR. I live for operations. Dr. Andersson really trained me. He waited several years—watched me, I guess. I worked for the hospital then. I was surprised when he asked me. I work as long as he does and hand him what he needs. I'm on salary." She takes great care on the job, and seems to me genuinely kind. She is a toucher and comforter of frightened patients, something rare in the many fearsome scenes I've witnessed. Doreen seems, ironically, the true heir of the motherly and wifely brand of professionalism Florence Nightingale brought to nursing more than a hundred years ago. But she is a survival, out of date in her contentment with her job as doctor's helper, reflecting an attitude born in an age when a woman who didn't "know her place" found no place at all in medicine. Some things in medicine have changed more slowly than others, and one of the slowest to change has been the attitude of most doctors toward women working with them. Unlike Doreen, many women in the field are not content merely to help out, however expertly. When nurses express their discontent, their assertion is that they "just want the liberty to do what we've been trained to do."

10

"Simplicity Isn't
Where We Are At Right Now"

About the time the first snow to stick whitened, then turned Andersson's mill city gray, he began to worry about his pacemaker patients. Within the space of a few months, half a dozen of their pacemakers—all of the brand he then favored—had failed. No one had died, but the set of events struck him as statistically ominous. Late one afternoon, after finishing with his surgery, office hours, and hospital rounds, Andersson sent Doreen home early and then spent several hours studying the records of these pacemaker patients, and discussing the meaning of their failures and the short, hot history of the industry in general.

During the 1970s, Andersson's pacemaker patients, and hundreds of thousands like them, constituted a growth industry. Their number grew with Medicare. It's mainly old people who get pacemakers, and the government paid for, and still pays for, most of them. The device was new, and so much in demand that some companies rushed each innovation into production while development was still under way. As pacemakers improved, daring companies with the "right" next innovation fattened, and conservatively managed companies got eaten. And an increasing range of patients became candidates for pacemakers. Recently, government hearings have shown that the pacemaker's popularity has exceeded its appropriate uses—that perhaps a fifth of pacemaker patients might do as well without them. Most everyone who needs one has one, and the only current demand—domestically, about 150,000 new ones were installed in 1982—comes from the newly ill. The European market isn't yet saturated. Third world markets, especially in countries with middle classes, still fascinate some manufacturers. But in the late sixties and early seventies, the stock of leading pacemaker companies (the largest, Medtronic, has held on to a major share of the market from the start) made the fortunes of early investors, including some surgeons.

Pacemaker sales were so lucrative, and the stakes so high, that manufacturers and some doctors led each other toward marketing practices that flirt with conflict of interest. One senior vascular surgeon told me, "The companies may not pay kickbacks, but frequently they give doctors very favorable treatment—gifts and junkets. 'Come see our factory,' they say, as if that's a medical necessity." Andersson said he had once toured a pacemaker factory, while already in the area at a medical conference. "No junket."

Most of the patients who have received pacemakers feel pleased with the promise of new life to come. But for a very few, dependence on a *machine*, on something chancy, manufactured, not really part of themselves, turns out to be an unbearable burden, a metaphor, perhaps, for the impositions of the age of technology upon private being. These few patients feel haunted by their pacemakers; the same thing (medical sociologist Renée Fox has reported) happens to some kidney dialysis patients, and Dr. Barney Clark, recipient of the world's first permanent artificial heart, was given not only the machine but also a key to turn the thing off. There's an eerie air of Faustian indiscretion to this technological continuing of life. The medical journals have published half a dozen articles identifying what they now code as "pacemaker twiddlers' syndrome." Usually it happens to older patients, ill with other diseases too, and feeling useless and hopeless, who become ambivalent about these artificial things that sustain them. They gouge their pacemakers out and pull them loose. Or they rotate them, working through the skin, spinning them until the lead wires part or dislodge. Surgeons have occasionally found such patients still alive, and when they operate, they relocate the pacemakers, sewing them securely and out of the way, under the groin, where they are harder to reach.

Most pacemaker patients come to terms with the devices, and it has become easier to do so with each year since their invention in the 1950s. "Everything that's in a pacemaker has been around for nearly thirty years," a colleague of Andersson's remarked. "It's just that it would have taken a room to hold all the equipment then, and now it all fits in the palm of my hand as I install it in a patient."

As pacemakers have shrunk, their longevity has increased. Pacemakers fall into the special category of space age paraphernalia designed to function in adverse environments, and with lives depending on their reliability. Bodies are wet, and acid, and a pacemaker has to do its deed right, a hundred thousand times a day. NASA jargon operant here is "Hi-Rel," and "pacer" engineers pride themselves on aerospace backgrounds.

By the mid-sixties, early pacemakers weighed nearly a pound—chiefly mercury batteries that had to be replaced in yearly surgery. The devices were hand-wired with transistor circuitry. They pulsed constantly at set frequency, sometimes aiding and sometimes interfering with the sick heart's surviving rhythms. The batteries often leaked and then failed. Nowadays pacemakers equipped with lithium batteries weigh just a few ounces and last for up to a decade. Tiny printed "hybrid" circuits give pacemakers new capabilities. A surgeon can reprogram a pacemaker's performance specifications, using a magnet and a control box, without operating. It can be reset to pulse more frequently, or more strongly, or upon less provocation, or only upon certain provocations—which is to say, pacemakers have grown more tactful. They even can report on their own functioning by telephone to computers that ignore good news but alert a doctor at the first sign of trouble.

Before the application of lithium batteries, at least one

manufacturer briefly turned out plutonium-powered pacemakers. A handful of patients still have them. The atomic pacemakers were distributed only after an environmental impact statement cleared the U.S. Atomic Energy Commission Fuels and Materials Directorate of Licensing. The "Risk Logic Model" from this statement includes a flow chart of "disposal outcomes" as complex as the catacombs. The chart speculates about what happens to the grain of deadly plutonium within each device when the "2.4×10^{-2} atomic pacemaker patients per 10,000" who the AEC asserted are destined to do so jump willfully from tall buildings. The chart knows. It graphs plutonium loss from patients in plane crashes, rail crashes, fires, explosions, and—most chillingly—from victims of "kidnap, homicide, and intentional removal of pacer." That's terrorists killing patients in order to snatch their atomic fuel. The elaborate chart is very fanciful—and praise the Lord for lithium batteries, which quickly halted production of atomic pacemakers. Andersson installed half a dozen of the atomic pacemakers when they were fashionable, and has one current patient. I met her one day. She was fortyish, active, and—like the crew of the *Nautilus* back in the 1950s—proud of her distinction. She spoke of the few similar patients around the country as "we" and wasn't about to trade in the machine that had returned her, years before, to life.

The batteries of lithium pacemakers last longer than the life expectancies of nearly all pacemaker patients. When they do fail, new pacemakers are engineered to signal their intentions. They lose strength, slow notably, but continue to function. Routinely, nowadays, pacemaker patients monitor battery function and heart rate by telephone. It's big business. Some cardiologists and vascular surgeons run their own phone monitor services or have special equipment and personnel in their offices for patients to visit frequently. Frank trade magazines talk about the income potential of such setups. Andersson leaves that part of the business to a large company in a neighboring state. His patients phone an "800" number every few weeks. Medicare usually pays a patient's fee. The patient holds both a special magnet and the telephone receiver up to the pacemaker, and the computer at the other end of the phone line asks the machine in the body what's going on. The system is full of "fail-safes," and usually works.

But occasionally, because of manufacturing problems or bad engineering, some brands of pacemaker have failed, or—in one well-publicized case—speeded up suddenly to hundreds of beats per minute, killing patients.

A pacemaker engineer for one small company commented to me about guarantees on the reliability of pacemakers: "Pacemakers are very reliable. The failures are few, but stand out, of course. The guarantees are a selling point. Our high-price model has a lifetime guarantee. That is some of the black humor of the pacer industry. It's easy to do. The pacer dies, and the patient dies. Now, with lithium batteries, everyone is giving what I call the Midas Muffler warranty—the Forever Pacer. The last pacer you'll ever need. Actually, experience shows, only about thirty percent will ever come back, and many that do will come back so far down the line that the interest on the money paid for the original will more than buy a replacement. What's more usual is that when a pacemaker does need replacement, the surgeon changes brands because the first brand no longer seems trustworthy to him. And no guarantee covers switching brands. The government pays for the new one, nine times out of ten, in those cases."

———————◆———————

Early in December, Andersson becomes certain that the brand of pacemaker he has been installing is untrustworthy. With his concern increasing by the second and a band of orderlies and nurses straggling after him, he dollies a cart, bearing an unconscious middle-aged man in brown pants and a plaid sweater, into the operating room of his hospital, moving at full tilt. A startled janitor, seeing this brigade rumble into the operating room, rushes toward a mop pail on wheels that stands filled with grayish water, in the far corner. Using the mop handle as a tiller, the janitor steers the pail out, banging his way past the entering cart.

Andersson is in galoshes—heavy, black, practical ones—and Doreen sports furry snow boots. The man in the brown pants aboard the cart still wears work shoes with thick cleated soles. His sweater bunches at the belly and his trousers gather at the knees. No one is dressed according to regulations; they defile this clean place. Two nurses set out to remedy this. The patient wakes up and watches, quietly. The nurses begin peeling back the plaid sweater, revealing a sleeveless ribbed undershirt beneath. Andersson moves in on the disrobing, shears in hand. He has the sweater and the undershirt converted into cardigan and vest before the litter is halted in place under the spotlights. Next layer: The surgeon begins cutting the skin of the bared chest. He's not bothering with anesthesia. In emergency situations, when moments count, surgeons may open abdomens, crack chests, reach for bleeding, for the heart, before anesthesia can be administered. This incision, opening the patient's pacemaker pouch, is trivial.

"I'm going again," the patient says softly. For the third time in ten minutes he passes out.

He had appeared in Andersson's office on time, just a few minutes before first fainting, for a routine annual follow-up visit. It is three years, nearly to the day, since Andersson implanted his pacemaker. He had come in, and had begun to tell the doctor his doubts—that he'd "felt fine until recently," then, that he'd "blacked out a few times two days ago," but that with his appointment so very near, he'd "just waited for it." Usually one goes off to the doctor only to find that all symptoms have evaporated. But with nearly fatal obligingness, this patient's pacemaker had sabotaged him again, on cue.

"It's happening," he had said, then had slumped forward, tottering as he'd sat, feet dangling, on the end of the examining table. Andersson had leaped toward him, had caught him and laid him down. Andersson had shouted for Doreen to call orderlies to come at once from the hospital. "Reserve an OR, emer-

135

gency!" he'd instructed her. He had listened to the patient's chest, and was still listening when the man had awakened.

"Did I have a heart attack?"

"Maybe not. I think your pacemaker has been giving you trouble. Relax. You're in the right place." The man had fainted again.

We'd heard the orderlies causing commotion—they couldn't get their cart through the narrow doorframe leading to Andersson's examining rooms, and they just stood near it, shouting and banging the cart against the opening now and then to demonstrate their difficulty.

"Take his legs," Andersson had said to me. Doreen rushed for the legs. I cradled the midsection, Andersson lifted under the arms, and we sidled down the narrow hall, sharing the weight. We had slid the patient, foot end first, through the hall doorway and up the length of the stretcher, which is when his pants and sweater had bunched up.

"We want to hurry," Andersson had said to the orderlies. We had hurried, Doreen pushing the feet, Andersson pushing the stretcher, and the orderlies striding at a near run next to the cart as it rolled, first out through the waiting room—where half a dozen old-timers looked on, aghast—and then down the corridor of the medical building.

Awakening again, on the cart, the patient must have felt his cold passage out the door, across the tar parking lot, and into the glass-walled hospital lobby, into the elevator, where the running stopped. He had fainted. We pushed his cart past the janitor, into the operating room.

———————◆———————

He awakens yet again at the first penetration of the knife.

"You're operating," he says. He sounds bewildered.

"It's a routine pacemaker incision," says Andersson, and he adds, as a quiet aside to Doreen, "and I'm hoping it's the pacer and not the lead."

Unbidden, the patient makes a muffled declaration, eyes

136

closed against the pain of the cut: "You have my permission to do whatever you have to do."

The incision is just a three-inch cut below the healed scar of the previous cut. Andersson hasn't stopped to scrub, or to suit up, but he has taken an instant to cram his hands into sterile gloves, and his arms through a surgical robe. This is the only time I ever see him operating without his big radio in the room. Within a minute he's exposed the steel-jacketed pacemaker, and a moment later, the lead wire extending downward from it into the chest. He loosens the lead wire. He quickly stabs a hypodermic needle in through the wire, and leaves it stuck there, dangling. Doreen hands him a plastic box, the size of a paperback dictionary, covered with knobs, dials, and switches. It's a temporary pacemaker, usually employed in initial installations to determine proper program settings. Andersson snaps the alligator clip on its cable onto the hypodermic needle that's stuck through the lead wire. He sets dials, flips the on switch.

It's like turning on Frankenstein's monster. The patient awakens. The patient smiles. You can see that he feels fine.

Andersson reacts with the aplomb of a championship bowler who rolls strikes but turns his back before the pins fly. He pauses to set things up right. A circulating nurse finally has shown up, ready to work. The staff is catching up with the action. He looks around, for the first time taking stock of the many departures from the protocols of asepsis. "Masks," he says, "gowns." A nurse reaches across Andersson's face and ties a mask around it. Perhaps he does smile in satisfaction the moment he is concealed. Nurses hold sterile gowns for each other, and take turns walking into them, arms held forward, like a crew of sleepwalkers at play. "Has intensive care been notified?" Doreen asks. The patient's shoes come off. Will they ever arrive in his hospital room upstairs? The cut sweater and brown pants submerge under green drapes. The patient watches through quiet blue eyes.

"Is the tension gone?" Doreen asks him.

"His or mine?" Andersson asks.

"Mine is, anyway," says the patient. He sounds zesty, even

corny. It's a voice from the other side; patients aren't supposed to join in staff quips. They are supposed to be knocked out, or at the very least groggy and befuddled. This man is jubilant. A whole two minutes past the probable moment of his death, he savors life, a miracle of electronics.

"Now you won't go out," Andersson tells him.

"Just make sure it's in tight," the patient says.

Doreen starts to scold the doubting patient, but Andersson stops her. "No," he says, holding up a hand with a scalpel in it. "He's had troubles like that a few years ago."

And the patient faints again, the blue eyes suddenly closing, face slackening.

Andersson jiggles the needle passing through the lead. He shakes it harder. Once more the patient awakens, in time to hear Andersson end a sentence, ". . . lousy contact."

"God, that's a horrible feeling. It feels like my whole head is exploding."

"You're back. You're O.K. now."

"Can I ask a stupid question?"

"No question is stupid."

"I just heard you say, 'lousy contact.'. . ."

"We made it happen," says Doreen, "and Doctor just fixed it. He wouldn't stop now if it wasn't O.K."

Andersson does not stop. An anesthesiologist puts in an appearance, and helps administer tranquilizer and local anesthetic. Andersson chooses a pacemaker from the hospital's inventory— one of a different brand. He's given up on the old brand. He regulates the settings, wires it into the existing lead, puts the old pacemaker aside.

"Can I have the old one?" the patient asks.

"Nope. It's going back to the company."

"I'll always need one. . . ."

"Yes, you'll always need a watchdog."

"Can't something be done?"

"This is basically all you need."

Obviously, as the patient has just learned by doing, this may not be basically all he needs. But it's all that's available, and once again, it works. The anesthesiologist regards the half-garbed crew, the alert patient, the jumble of wires, the black box, clips and forceps spread across the disorganized drapes. He shakes his head, and says, "Simplicity isn't where we are at right now."

———◆———

In a wonderful way, Andersson is doing something here very different from an orthopedist installing even as sophisticated a hinge as an artificial knee joint, or a heart surgeon installing a plastic valve. The seemingly libidinal undertones to Andersson's musing, "A good surgeon puts a part of himself into every patient he operates on," take on a new and cerebral resonance here. It's as if he's installing a bit of his own brain. The new thing about the current generation of pacemakers that makes them different from other surgical devices is that they react. They represent the patient's best interests under changeable conditions. With each beat of the heart, the pacemaker repeats a question: "You got an R wave of your own, dear heart? Do you need me this time?" Seventy times a minute, a hundred thousand times a day, it's "Sweet heart, do you need me now?"

Whenever the answer is no, the machine saves electricity for one beat. Then it asks again. Whenever the answer is yes, it helps out.

"May I now?"

Zap.

"May I now?"

Zap.

"May I now?" (No.)

Pause.

Such persistent and invasive dutifulness has never before been known. It's as if a little Jewish mama surgeon stays behind to continue doing right by the patient after the surgeon closes.

———◆———

The debt incurred by a patient in exchange for such a gift of life may not be apparent, to either surgeon or patient, at first. The doctor gets paid—and it's worth speculating whether surgeons' high billings may be tolerated by consumers in part because, when the work does succeed, the value of life preserved far exceeds the billing of even the poshest society surgeon.

Writing about organ transplants, Renée Fox describes the relationship between donor and recipient. Her observations apply, although sometimes more mildly, to relationships in general between patients whose lives have been saved and their surgeons. "[It] is inherently unreciprocal. There is a fundamental sense in which the recipient can never totally repay the donor."

Once, a patient Andersson had returned to vigor and employment by installing a pacemaker in him saved up for a year, and then just before Christmas, walked into the hospital and handed the administrator six new hundred-dollar bills. "He told me," the administrator explained to Andersson later that afternoon, "to keep five of these bills for the hospital, and to give this one to you." Andersson had laughed and shaken his head in delight, and folded the new hundred-dollar bill into his wallet.

A state of incuriosity, and of less manifested gratitude, seems more usual for pacemaker patients—even where wariness and curiosity about the device might better serve the patient's interests. Pacemaker companies provide surgeons with comprehensible advisory manuals—full of charts and illustrative cardiograms, well explained. They are designed so that even the most ill-informed, anciently trained surgeon can learn from them—and also will be led to conclude that the only medically responsible thing to do is keep prescribing the pacemaker manufactured by whatever company has issued his guidebook.

The pacemaker installed in the man with brown slacks and plaid sweater came with a second booklet as well—"A New Way of Life," a twenty-four-page glossy production with a fetching close-up of a butterfly on its cover. It's the patient's author's manual. Like similar brochures from other pacemaker companies, this one reads with the sweet hush-now-dear style usually reserved for fundamentalist sex education pamphlets and the fliers squeezed into every junior tampon package. They all illustrate with butterflies.

This tract is—seemingly inevitably—in the question-and-answer format that makes the answers comforting, and authoritative, like a nice dull day in kindergarten.

Brochures such as this must be most patients' only printed information on the new creatures that guard their lives. Yet mauve cartoon drawings sport through the Qs and As.

Q: Why Do I Need A Pacemaker?
A: . . . your body has its own electrical system. [butterfly]
Q: What Else Do I Need To Know? [butterfly]
A: Your doctor will be happy to answer the questions you may have. . . .

The payoff question, fitted carefully around a big blue hovering monarch, comes late in the booklet.

Q: Can My Pacemaker Fail?
A: Yes, but the possibility of this happening is remote. The years of research and testing spent by pacemaker manufacturers *has* minimized this possibility. Pacemakers are manufactured under the same rigid quality controls developed for the space program. . . . [butterfly]

Returning to his office after operating, Andersson looks preoccupied. He pulls from his pocket the pacemaker that failed, and rolls it over a few times in his hand. "I guess God decided to stop pulling the rug this fellow was standing on," he says. He slips in the rear door of the office. Looking down the hall, over the receptionist's back, and out past the counter in front of her, he can see that the patients in the waiting room still wait. He ignores them. He is upset, angry. His step is resolute. As he strides into his office he says to the receptionist, "Get me Jimmy Manwell on the phone, now. It's time to do something."

He eases into his desk chair and waits, looking down, saying nothing. A few minutes later, the phone buzzes.

"Jimmy? Danny Andersson . . . Not too bad . . . Listen, the situation we've been following of premature battery troubles? I'd say your company is in trouble. Second time in two weeks now—one just dumped. Didn't fade. *Dumped. Suddenly—no warning.*" Andersson's voice has gotten clipped, strained, sarcastic. I've never heard him like this. "His last phone check—just two weeks ago—was fine. This one went suddenly, with intermittent cardiac arrest. We just caught him. It was unbelievable, but he happened to be in the office at the time. Any more like that and there's going to be a total hold on your product in this area." That threat sounds mild to me.

A few weeks later, there is indeed another one like that— caught sooner, and with less drama because the patient is not completely pacemaker-dependent. Afterward, Andersson informs all three hundred or so patients in whom he has installed this brand that they should step up telephone monitoring. As they come in for routine examinations, every quarter or half year, he begins a policy of proposing to all that their pacemakers, although guaranteed for longer wear, be removed by the end of the third year of use.

He ceases his habit of installing only one brand, and decides to spread his unusually large volume of business around more. If his hundred new pacemaker patients a year buy units that wholesale for $5,000 (never mind still larger operating and hospital fees), that's half a million dollars' worth of business a year for pacemaker manufacturers that depends entirely on Andersson's discretion. He ceases installing the troublesome brand altogether. This means that no patient benefits from the guarantee the brand offered, which allows for replacement by the company.

Laboratory examination of the malfunctioning pacemakers shows, eventually, that the trouble is with a bad lot of batteries. Corroborating data are organized by one of the large telephone monitoring companies, working closely with Andersson. The trouble with the brand turns out to be quite general. Other doctors have reported difficulties too. Some months after these suspicions are confirmed, an article appears in *PACE*—the trade journal of the industry—and notification on the "gray sheets" of the Food and Drug Administration publicizes the problem still more widely, although the *PACE* article lists the battery lots, rather than the brand, so only insiders gather this crucial news. The company, pressured by several angry surgeons to refrain from selling out their entire remaining inventory of the model in question, suffers severe financial distress.

In the ensuing year, Andersson's rate of pacemaker installation doubles. A hundred replacement procedures. In most cases, he is able to collect government or insurance company fees for the reoperations. In the few cases where the burden of payment falls directly on patients, he refrains from charging for his services. The volume of extra surgery and extra pacemaker sales constitutes a windfall for his hospital, which follows standard practice in attaching a markup of about a hundred percent to all surgical devices it sells. It also seems to be a windfall for Andersson, although one he receives as a mixed blessing. Even the private insurers, whose payout increases infinitesimally because of this incident, adjust their fees upward accordingly. The loss is diffuse, widely shared by those carrying medical insurance. Taxpayers lose by the slight rise in Medicare payments.

The manufacturers of the defective pacemakers, of course, lose—although they and their insurers are rumored to be seeking damages from their battery supplier (who probably also has insurance for such occasions). The many hundreds of affected patients across the country are losers, subjected to extreme danger, anxiety, pain, and time sick. Finally, the small group of backers who bankrolled the pacemaker company—several of whom prove to be surgeons—also lose on their private investments. By the end of a year's time, Andersson's rate of pacemaker surgery returns to his normal hundred a year. None of his patients have lost their lives, although there have been a few close calls. It is a year the patients, their surgeon, the manufacturer, and the investors are all glad to put behind them.

143

11

"It Is Sad to See Such a Terrible Problem Thrust Upon Them"

I asked Andersson once why he had chosen the field of vascular surgery, when it seemed far more predictable and confined than general surgery. "No cancer," he'd answered. "Vascular surgeons never deal with cancer. I think I saw one case of vascular cancer when I was a resident. It almost doesn't happen."

Stearne, on the other hand, sees cancer all the time. He's used to it, and he's even proud of his ability to defy the terror of it. "I think my partner and I must have more cured cancer patients running around town," he says one day in early winter, "than any other surgical practice around here does." I feel trapped by the boast. I will have to see what he sees if I stick around. I've seen enough already: uncles, aunts, grandmothers, friends, and my very nice ex-mother-in-law.

I stick around. Every week a few cancer patients, some cured, visit Stearne's office. Then one week he announces, "I have an interesting series of appointments. There's a professor from the law school—came in through the HMO. He's had a five-year battle with cancer. They took out a perforated colon cancer to begin with, then more and more surgery, including some heroic surgery. He was working in spite of his disease for most of that time. Now he has a resurgence all over. Nothing to do for him anymore.

"Also, I have down a plastics engineer. A rare bile-duct cancer. May be job-related. It's hard to tell in these cases. He won't make it, either.

"And then there's a schoolteacher—she has cancer too. Stomach cancer. Knows what's going on. Her internist doesn't usually send me patients. But he's one of those people who does send me patients he cares for especially."

"Did the internist diagnose her?"

"She came in to me thinking she had a stomach ulcer."

"Does she have a chance?"

"About zero. That's what the long-term studies show. But some recent studies show that chemotherapy may possibly do some good. I'm going to discuss it with her."

"Will it really help?"

"Some, perhaps—for a while. But who knows? She may be a first. There's also a boy with Hodgkin's disease. He's number one on the list for this afternoon."

"You must look at these difficult visits with some dread?" I ask.

"I'm not to blame," he exclaims, quite intently. "I'm not the one who gave them cancer. I've done them good, in fact. Kept them alive. I feel good to see them, knowing there's a chance that I can help."

A giant of a teenager walks into the office, as big around as the trunk of an old maple. He's wearing gray sweat pants and sweat shirt, as if he's just come from doing roadwork.

"How's the truckdriving business?" Stearne asks as the boy opens the office door.

"Good, I guess," he answers slowly. His face, broad and red, stays expressionless. He's beyond reach of Stearne's professional manner.

"He has a couple of rocks in his neck," Stearne explains. The boy sits down. Stearne wheels his office chair forward a yard and feels the right side of the boy's neck, confirming his memory of the condition. "Remember," he asks, addressing the boy, "the last time, I told you there was a possibility that you had Hodgkin's disease? Hodgkin's has changed"—it doesn't ap-

145

pear to me that the boy understands, nor that the doctor is speaking to be understood—"and I think the probability is that you do have Hodgkin's disease. Now, eighty-five percent of the people who we see who get it, get over it completely, through X-rays, and medicine—"

A ringing phone interrupts the presentation. I wonder how Stearne, with a hundred or so cancer patients in various stages of learning their fates, fighting, raging, accepting, keeps track of the delicate progress of these hundred relentless narratives. Stearne remains on the phone for a full five minutes, arguing with some bureaucratically powerful nurse. The boy stares out the window and doesn't twitch a muscle. It seems Stearne has dictated yesterday's incoming-patient reports after the closing time stipulated by hospital regulation for new admissions. The nurse wishes to remove the name of a patient from the next day's surgery roster. Stearne is polite, claiming that he was on hold, awaiting his turn to dictate the admitting information, at three minutes before deadline, and that he appreciates the nurse's help in keeping things just as they are. He finally hangs up, assured that, just this once, she will make an exception for him.

"—and a bit of tissue from your neck, I think, and that hard gland under your arm there, would make it diagnostic. Also, the further you get from the source, into the armpit, the more your symptoms tend to be diagnostic—"

The patient still looks uncomprehending, unshaken, inert. Stearne notices. "You have a treatable cancer," he says. "Cancer of the lymph glands, I suspect. We need to get you in for a biopsy. The nurse can schedule it out there for you." He points out into the hallway.

"O.K.," says the boy, getting up. He grips the office door, then, holding on to it, asks, "You want this door shut or leave it open?"

Why can't he slam it, trap the bad news inside? I admire his defenses. This is the moment he hears that fate has turned on him. I ask Stearne about his own feelings: Does it bother him, telling the boy that kind of news?

"I tell maybe fifty patients a year that they have cancer—usually breast or colon. I didn't give it to him. It doesn't have emotional impact on me. I probably cure more than I don't. The patients get more of a charge out of it than I do."

"What if you were in the patient's shoes, and another doctor were giving you the news that *you* had cancer?"

"I don't know how I'd feel. Probably about the same as I feel telling them they have it."

Can it be that to be professionalized is to lose touch with all fear, all sense of the desperate sweetness of life? Can one become so mechanistic in comprehending one's own somaticism that one might actually *have* cancer dispassionately? And how long might the dispassion endure? Past the first ten pounds of weight loss? Twenty? Fifty? It's as if you might live on and on if only you can keep from noticing. For a few years, a late senior partner of Stearne's assisted in operations upon cancer patients, all the while keeping his own prostate cancer in check with hormonal treatments. The partner's insularity, like Stearne's, was awesome.

The law professor is in next, quickly seated in the armchair by the window. He and the truckdriver must have passed each other in the corridor, both lost in their own concerns. Did either notice the other? The professor is stooped, gray-haired and gray-skinned, curled in on himself in the bright-green chair—a garden snail on a leaf. He looks up at Stearne through groggy eyes, only half engaged by this late chapter of an old ordeal. There's nothing more to do. The questions that come from Stearne are kindly ones, about how he's doing, and if he's comfortable, and does he need or wish anything. "You can call me anytime," Stearne says. The professor just nods, and then he's gone, out through the open door, dying on his own now.

The receptionist says the plastics engineer has rescheduled for tomorrow. I'm glad. One fewer.

Later, the teacher with stomach cancer comes in. Rather, she slips in sideways, as if entering a lecture late, hoping not to be noticed while things go on normally, as they must have before her illness. She is powerful, imploding with the force of new terror. She returns nothing to the outer world as she moves in slowly, wide-eyed and stoop-necked. Stearne studies her appearance, and who knows what he thinks. My thoughts fly out toward her and fragment, gone. She's very thin. She says, quietly, "Can't keep food down." She makes an apologetic shrug. It's the only thing she says. She folds into the easy chair.

Her husband has walked in behind her, a big, sandy-haired man, a fireman. He doesn't touch her or look at her. He sits across the room and squints. "I traded time with someone so I could make it after all," he says. They have two kids. "Kluzko," he says, introducing himself, wrapping a hand like a rolled roast around the doctor's.

On Stearne's desk is a letter from a surgeon in Boston:

> I saw your nice young patient, Bea Kluzko, in consultation on Wednesday. She and her husband are certainly most delightful and pleasant people, and it is sad to see such a terrible problem thrust upon them. . . . The diagnosis is poorly differentiated adenocarcinoma of the stomach.

The cancer is gone now, along with the rest of the stomach. Stearne has told me that after removing the mass, he searched and found no visible metastases—"no macroscopic spread," is how he put it—but that he had taken little reassurance from that fact, because of the sort of tumor he found. "The numbers aren't good," he said to me. "They give us little reason to hope."

What he tells her now, however, is that a five-year study of adjuvant chemotherapy in gastrointestinal cancer has "given good evidence that we benefit people by giving this chemotherapy." He tells her she's fortunate, because an oncologist, a tumor expert, who helped in that very study lives in a city just half an hour away.

She doesn't ask him about the therapy; she doesn't even ask what he means by "benefit people." She's doing battle with the real issue. She nods a nod of assent so slight it might have been just an isolated tremor. Stearne says, "I'll have the oncologist's office call tomorrow to schedule a first visit," and she slips back out of the office, followed by her husband.

———————

Then Stearne calls the oncologist. He carefully describes the patient and her disease, then stresses her youth, her children, her career, her happy marriage, and he tells the oncologist he plans to suggest chemotherapy to her. The oncologist may be resisting the idea that he can help, because Stearne says, "What else can we do?" The oncologist must finally be persuaded. "Then you'll call her tomorrow? Good."

Stearne dictates his record of her visit at once. It ends with the curious sentence: "Prognosis is, of course, guarded." The prognosis is, of course, death. And what is actually guarded is Stearne.

Still later, I follow Stearne into an examining room. He sees a man who got kicked by a horse. He sees a newlywed, examines her breasts and tells her that the lumps she has felt there do not alarm him.

My ear alarms me. I have thought about it now and then for a month or two, and it scares me, right now. I have a small disturbance of the skin, right on the upper tip of the left ear. It looks pearly in the mirror, like a spot of acne twenty years behind the times. Since I first noticed it, it has gotten slightly larger, birthed a tiny calf next to it, and it hurts when I sleep on it, although not very much. I've planned vaguely to mention it to the family doctor sooner or later.

Now, in the middle of Stearne's dreadful series of patients, I touch my ear, remember my anxiety, and violate a rule of work I have long followed: I stop being whatever Stearne makes of me and become a patient. May I steal a minute of your time too? Yes. Would you look at my ear? Certainly. He points to the stool under the strong lamp, and as I sit, starts to dial the telephone. He holds a receiver in one hand and tugs at my ear with the other, aligning my head so he can see well.

149

"Yup, cancer. You got cancer," he says. "Hello, dear," he says into the phone. He chats on the phone while I wait, about when it would be convenient to admit some patient to the hospital. He flirts with the "dear" on the other end. I start to write down what he says so I can show how he flirts. Instead I write down how I feel just then, because the first moment of detachment passes, and I know it's me who has cancer. The hair on the back of my neck stands straight out; I feel it rising. My notes:

1. Dissociation. Oh, he's just making another comment.
2. Numbness.
3. Go bugeyed, start breathing heavily, and panic.

The panic is firmly installed by the time Stearne hangs up the phone and grabs the ear again. I'm a patient now; he addresses not me but the attending nurse. "Classic. Basal cell. Wrong age, wrong place, for squamous. See the pearl color, the teardrop shape? And it's in a location that is subject to these lesions from sunlight. Classic."

"So that's what it looks like?" I hear the nurse remark to him.

"Tell me something reassuring," I say. I laugh nervously, to show him I'm a sport. I'm still looking nearly directly into the hot, bright examining lamp.

Dr. Stearne lets go of my ear. I turn toward him. "I'm ashamed of you," he says to me. "You really are neurotic. I thought you were a medical insider now. Don't you know the body's just a machine and it breaks down every once in a while?"

"This is *my* body breaking. You've just told me I have cancer."

"Skin cancer. Nobody dies from skin cancer."

"What do I do?"

"Come into the office tomorrow, when I have more time, and I'll take a biopsy, just to confirm it. I'm pretty sure it is. Next week you'll have an answer—we'll get the results on Monday or Tuesday. Then we'll cut it out. Just a little spot. Then maybe we'll need to freeze it, or electrocauterize the area too."

"It doesn't spread?"

"Not basal cell. It's probably basal cell. Your age, the location. Squamous looks the same. That one sometimes spreads."

I say nothing. I feel foggy, far off, askew from the body sitting bolt upright in the chair by the light and the examining table.

The next patient comes in. My notes say:

Tall, gangly, red-haired male student. Friendly. Has
boil on sinewy leg. Treated topically. Surgeon shows
restraint.

After the boy leaves, I come to my senses. I decide (as patient advocates recommend nowadays) to take control of the situation. "Russ Stearne," I say, "I want you to do me a favor. You've known me for over a year, and you'd have to call me an anxious sort, probably, insider or not. I want you to take the biopsy now. I want you to put it in a specimen jar, and I'll take it over to the hospital lab myself. I want you to mark it 'Rush,' and I'll hope to get an answer tomorrow, and not to have to wait through the weekend."

Stearne shrugs the sort of shrug I've seen him use on old persons too thick to understand the obvious. Like them, I ignore it. He shakes his head, and his palms rise. "I know what it is already. Don't you trust your doctor?" He's teasing me about the shift in roles. I regret it already. "It's just skin cancer. Don't worry about it." I still look worried about it. He shrugs again, this time a shrug of consent.

"Here, sit down on this table. Put your legs up. Now lie on your right side." I've heard these mechanical orders often, and have watched impassively while patients' bodies have moved into position for examination. He swings the harsh lamp back over to the burning ear.

"It's not anything I'd worry about," he says. After the line-up of cancer patients, and Stearne's dispassionate reception of them, I take little comfort in knowing what he wouldn't worry about. I think of saying so, but suddenly feel docile, whipped. I elect politeness. *I* know the diplomacy of survival.

"I'm not cutting you," he says, coming at me with a syringe of novocaine, and then with a pair of scissors. Oh, he remembers all our old chats. "This may sting." I've heard it before. He injects. It doesn't sting much. I think of writing this passage, and wonder if I will write it in the midst of a struggle against dying.

He cuts. "I fix people," he says as he cuts, still quoting himself. I hear the sound of gristle dividing against the edge of the blade. He readjusts the light. It's stronger in my closed eye. I feel only a tugging at the ear. I hear the cutting sound again.

I feel elated at being treated. I feel elated.

"I took them both right away. In the jar." I unsquint my eyes and sit up. He's writing on the tag attached to a squat jar. The tag says Rush.

I'm too bleary to rush. I climb down slowly from the table, as Stearne's patients do. I touch gauze and tape on the ear, and smell the fresh adhesive smell. In the jar the devil looks tiny, curled in on itself, afloat, drowned succubus. I walk out, thanking him, jar in hand, through a waiting room filled with more patients. I'd rather be carrying a fecal sample in Macy's parade.

I drop the jar, tied round with its label, at the lab. I have become the loathed thing. The test may come back tomorrow, they tell me there, and then again it may take the weekend. We are busy here. I drive home. Yesterday I felt the false pride of being the doctor's pal. Today I know the score; I'm nobody special. Cancer comes like the common cold. One breath away from health, achoo, and the ordeal, the long ordeal, is started. It's as easy as a sneeze.

I don't mind the death part. What scares me is the process of hopelessness, of having no prospects, of progressive incapability frustrating ambition. I repent my every wasted moment. I eat supper without tasting, and make life hard for everyone around. I phone the family doctor and she confirms that I'm "overdramatizing"—that even if it proves to be cancer, it is indeed almost certainly basal cell, and, indeed, she's never heard of anyone dying from it who has caught it this early, or even much later.

I can't desist, though. I dream awful dreams in spite of strong drink and kind words. By now I'm not mourning just the particulars of my case, but the awful prospect of cancer; it's a burden of modern times, the internal equivalent of nuclear war. The first skirmish has started. Cancer kills one in four, I read. One man in eighteen loses a lung. One woman in fourteen, a breast. Colons go, stomach, bladders, testes, the blood, pancreases, livers, ears. Death stew.

By the light of day, I listen to reason. I calm down. Stearne calls with a mean temptation. While we talk I'm aware that I'm jealous of him because he's growing wholesome cells only. He says, "I've got a lung to do first thing tomorrow morning." I say I'll be there; I've never seen chest surgery. I'll just hang on to my hat and go right back to work, I think.

Then it's later and I'm on my way, blank, detached, wary. In the hospital corridor, the hospice posters mean me, not my ex-wife's poor mother. I feel as if I'm visiting surgery for the first time and not the hundredth.

———————

"It's bloody, going into chests," Stearne says. "On the way in there's well-vascularized tissue." The patient lies on her side, knocked out, with a table of tools swung out right over her head. She's sunk in anesthesia, buried in green cotton. A teardrop section of rib cage shows through the draping, swabbed the familiar Betadine orange. Stearne has begun below the woman's breast, cutting a sweeping curve along the contour of a rib, ending halfway down the left side of her back.

He cuts not with a knife but with the electric scalpel that cauterizes as it cuts. The room, to my regret, soon smells of steak. "This makes things neater until we get through the area here filled with all these small blood vessels—they tend to be a little messy," Stearne says over the sparking of the device. "There, now we're going through the latissimus dorsi, the wide muscles of the back . . ." He puts two rubber-clad fingers under the wide muscles of the back, draws the muscles up away from the underlying surface, and cuts through them. As blood oozes, he clamps and stitches the cut vessels. He looks around. His gaze settles on the tamest, oldest nurse.

"Charlene, how long does pulmonary surgery usually take?" He asks the question with a baby-faced grin.

Charlene shrugs. Other nurses, caught in his gaze in turn, shrug. His partner, Culver, shrugs satirically. Even the anesthesiologist, staying out of trouble up at the end of the table, shrugs. Another shrug fest. Stearne is meeting with resistance.

"Three hours, frequently, doesn't it?" he asks the nurse.

"I suppose. It depends on the kind of pulmonary surgery, Doctor." Her answer will have to do.

"Well, this is going to take an hour and a half." He dissects inward, buzzing, stitching, deepening the smile he's drawn across the absent patient.

"This is the rhomboid muscle, attached to the scapula," Stearne mutters. After a while he moves to the other end of the incision, ". . . and this is the serratus muscle." He again forces his gloved left hand under muscle, then halves the separated fascia with the cautery. "My partners and I have a lot of patients walking around town cured of cancer," he says.

"Yesterday was her birthday," says the anesthesiologist, looking up from his charts. I imagine the wistful comments that must have been exchanged in her hospital room last night.

"We usually take a rib out to do this. In this case"—Stearne pauses and counts ribs—"it's the fifth rib." With a sculptor's tool, a long-handled blunt chisel, he strips flesh from the candidate rib. Three firm slides of the tool and it's clean white bone. He works the chisel through the cartilage at the rib's chest end. He holds the rib up.

"Spare rib," he says, laying it on the specimen cart.

"There isn't much meat on it," the anesthesiologist says, cheerily. I remember, again, the ability of anesthetized patients to register what is said in the operating room.

With the rib out, her lung shows, pale purple, like the skin of a boiled tongue, and as shiny as if it had been waxed and buffed.

Stearne lays down the chisel and the cautery, and reaches his hand, knuckles up, through the slot into the chest. He slides his fingers far up along the inside of the chest wall, toward whatever has made the shadow on the X-ray that hangs on the wall across the room.

Then, in a flat voice, a tone laden with disappointment and guardedness, he says, "Ooh, boy. This tumor has gone up into the chest wall."

It's a verdict. The prisoner shows no emotion. She is fitted with a rib spreader. It resembles a large woodworker's clamp, F-shaped and a foot long. A crank and gearing are built into the middle intersection, and prongs come out from the extremities of each crosspiece, like the legs of a trivet. Stearne fits the prongs of one crosspiece against the fourth rib, and the prongs of the other against the sixth rib. He cranks. The jaws spread, and the opening in her body, mail-slot sized, doubles in width. An elegant tool. It's easy to see more lung now, and easier to take stock. He reaches back up to feel the tumor again.

"This may not be operable at all," he says. "You got blood?" he asks the anesthesiologist. "If I take it out, it might be bloody. It comes right over to the aorta." He's feeling, reporting, working his hand in, feeling farther in. He shakes his head, draws his hand out, and sighs.

On the face of the upper lobe of the exposed lung, I see hundreds of black dots, as if someone had dabbed a fountain pen again and again against purple blotting paper. I ask about them.

"Carbon particles."

"That's not the cancer?"

"No, anyone who smokes has lungs like this. Also anyone who lives near a factory, or beside a busy road. Anyone who works in smoky areas, or where there's carbon dust. Anyone who lives in a city. Environmental pollution looks like this."

155

I look closely at the black spots. I wonder if the goals of environmental preservation would be more easily accomplished were we all transparent, like tropical fish—if our purple lungs showed their every foul soot spot right through glassy skin.

Stearne's partner, Culver, reaches in and feels the tumor. Stearne feels the tumor more, and describes what he finds for Culver's verification: "The tumor surrounds the upper lobe and impinges on the artery there. Also on the aorta. Also on the chest wall. The inter-lobar fissure is complete." Culver nods. Stearne thinks, and says decisively, "I am going to take the bulk of it out. If the arteries and veins are encased in tumor, you can't. At least in her case the artery isn't."

"I'm starting a unit of blood," the anesthesiologist says, "and, let's see, pressure reading, one-ten."

Stearne cuts, deep in the wound. He begins the resection in earnest. He's focused, civil, at his tamest when in action. He talks constantly to Culver as he works. "I can get a tie around here. . . . Yes. . . . This will be a palliative operation. She'll have radiation too. . . . Let's see if I can get a little more, distally . . . a clip for there. . . . I think there's a big patch under there . . . yes. . . . Maybe it'll be better using this. . . . Artery's good around here. . . . I've got to find the other branch now. . . . Theoretically, without this lobe she'll stand X-ray therapy better because there'll be less broken-down flesh for the body to cart away. . . . I can get to the end of that. . . . "

Culver, who has been assisting inside the wound, snipping sutures, probing and shoving tissue in order to display work better for Stearne, interrupts the monologue. "It's a total loss," he says. "Too much tumor." It's the first time he's spoken.

Stearne backs up and pauses. He looks over at the nurse who wouldn't tell him how long pulmonary surgery takes, and asks her a new question: "How are you, Charlene?"

"Fine."

"That's good, because if you weren't, it would ruin my day."

He has the lung freed of most of its attachments. He folds it up out of the wound and invites me to inspect, gesturing into the cleared opening, like a host leading a guest into the parlor, graciously. The incision now is a foot and a half long, half a foot wide, and a foot deep. In past the frame of the F-clamp, the gauze-cloaked sidewalls slope toward a pink, pulsing floor.

"That's the pericardium at the bottom, with the heart just inside it, making it bounce."

The pericardium shakes with sharp, healthy pulses. It is veined, like a leaf. Its rhythm matches the peeps of the anesthesiologist's heart monitor. The abstracted sound I've heard on every hospital visit for a year signals this throbbing flesh. I back away, listening.

"It's a very normal beat," the anesthesiologist says, and sings along: "Ta-deet, ta-deet, ta-deet." According to the clock on the wall, we are an hour into the operation. According to Stearne, we have half an hour to go.

He takes up his monologue again: "Now then, this *is* one large branch going down there. . . . Do you have a fine stitch to put into the pulmonary artery? . . . There, you're O.K., yes. . . . We control all arteries to the lower lobes, then the veins. . . . Over here the lobes aren't connected together by tumor . . . yes, they're not. . . . That's easier than when they're stuck together by lung cancer. In a case like that, though, a surgical stapler can quickly develop a fissure between the lobes. That's one good use for it. . . . O.K., let's flip the lobe over. . . . " The tumorous lobe, dangling from a tongs, comes up out of the incision further.

I see the cancer.

It's smog yellow, and it lurks just under the surface of the lung, smeared around in patches, like skin-covered cottage cheese. Stearne clips in around the strands of tissue that still tie the lobe into the lung, right down at the edge of the pericardium. In a moment, the lobe is attached by only one thin strip of tissue. He draws the lobe well clear of the wound. I can see across the arch of the chest interior to the far wall of the rib cage. The surgical lamps glow down through the skin. The view across the interior is like looking up at the arches and spokes of a pink beach umbrella.

Stearne points to the strand of lung running into the wound

from the nearly severed lobe. "Is this anything important, Char-lene?" he asks. "Is it O.K. if I tie and cut this thing here when I don't know what it is?" He cuts. "Have you any 3–0, Char-lene?"

Charlene passes along 3–0. Stearne stitches. Charlene gin-gerly lifts the detached lobe of lung with a tongs and drops it into a stainless steel pan. She carries the pan away from the operating table, to the small cart by the door. I walk over to look. The lobe sits next to the rib. As I watch, it hisses, like a cut tire, sagging, losing life.

The same noise seeps from the severed bronchus, inside the patient, where the lobe joined the next lobe down. Stearne closes the breach with more 3–0, and says to the anesthesiologist, "O.K., hyperventilate the patient." He spills a gallon jug of warmed saline solution into the patched chest cavity and stands watching the pooled water, alert for bubbles that would indicate leakage of air. When he's sure she's airtight, he drains the chest with an aspirator, then closes.

Stearne relaxes. His shoulders unhunch. "Many people don't have too much pain from this operation," he says, "but it's variable."

"Official name of operation for the form?" a nurse asks. Behind her, two other nurses count sponges, then needles.

"Left upper lobectomy." The incision, stitched up, looks like two enormous pursed lips, beaming at the surgeon. He says, to no one in particular, "Taking out the tumor won't affect the length of survival. It may make her more comfortable. It will stop her from being short of breath; tumor infiltrated the lobe we removed, so that blood pumped in there didn't oxygenate. Now all the lung she has will oxygenate blood for a while. Lung cancer is very bad."

Charlene is crawling around the floor at Stearne's feet. "I dropped a needle," she says. She finds it, by a leg of the table. She groans getting back on her feet, and sighs, "I'm getting old."

Unburied from the draping, the patient is eased from table to cart. Her rib and lung leave the room on their own cart, draped now as if the cargo were a whole tiny cadaver. We follow in a line as the patient is wheeled down the hall to the recovery room. New nurses—among those in the hospital with the greatest opportunity to exercise their skill freely—flurry around the bed as it rolls in to the recovery room. Stearne hands one the intravenous jars he's held aloft during the short journey. The patient awakens quickly, and must, somewhere in her filling mind, hear a nurse, a big, sweating, red-haired nurse, talking quietly into her ear: "We're going to be all around you, honey. You want your blanket pulled up? Is your hand hurting? There's tubes in it is all."

———————

A while later, Stearne meets me in the hospital parking lot. "Guess what?" he says. "You don't have cancer. I've been to pathology." Once again it takes half a minute for me to know it's really me he's talking about. I invite friends in for supper and celebrate with champagne. I smile for three days running. But things are changed; I feel the logic of the full-time healers' armor. It makes more sense. To remain raw to the chanciness of life is to remain in mourning. After a week of doubt, my life is recreated. A toast to the doers.

———————

Stearne offers more cancer surgery. I'm eager to go, and when I do, the room seems less exotic, and more humdrum than it ever has before. Today it's a workshop with good tools, with craft going on. Wheel in the job, check the work order that comes along with it, fix things as well as they can be fixed, and on to the next. The jokes seem mild, a handy way to relieve the pressures of a long workday. Old guy who's rich asks young girl to marry him. What about sex? she says. In-frequently, he says. That one word or two? she says. On the table, another incision develops, getting down to more business.

The patient is a mild, gray-haired man not yet sixty. He

159

appeared trim and pleasant when I met him the previous evening. His X-ray now hangs in a lightbox behind the table. The shadow of the real thing, on film, leaves the malice of the disease unannounced. Only the gross trouble shows, and the patient's fate depends on details, on millimeters' difference of location, on the timing of the accident of discovery.

Stearne returned to the hospital after office hours yesterday to study this film. He visited with the radiologist, then went upstairs to see the patient. The man's head and hands shook as Stearne talked about what the films show. "As we mentioned in the office, it is a tumor, it is in the lower bowel, and it is about a foot above the anus. From this new X-ray, it does look small and easy to remove. We'll take six inches of intestine on either side of it, and join the remaining bowel together—you'll still have a colon, just it'll be a little shorter. If things are as they appear to be, no colostomy. You'll never miss that section. Looks good."

"I can't understand it," Stearne said once we were out in the corridor. "I don't know why he shook like that after I told him it looked O.K. I still don't think I'd react like that." This time, I believe him. He's got it all stored away, maybe for keeps. The patient and I are sentient apples; Stearne's a sentient orange. Takes all types. Judge not. He gets the job done.

In the operating room, Stearne has dissected down to the site of the shadow. He grabs hold of the loop of gut harboring the offending tumor and feels it.

"It's contained," he announces. "This feels favorable." He works it with his fingers. "It's easy to mobilize. There are no attachments. It isn't through the wall of the intestine. I can't see it now, and that's a *very* good sign." He reaches up, then, under the intestines, and feels the lobes of the liver, where bowel cancer usually migrates, where bad news might still announce itself. He searches the liver with his fingers, and as he searches, he glances up over his shoulder, catching the eye of one of the younger nurses, one he knows cares especially about the fate of patients, and he says, "There appear to be no metastases present, left lobe, and . . . none present, right lobe. It's clean." No sighs of relief, but everyone smiles. The eyes of masked faces do look nice.

A life is being saved. A newcomer might not see the rejoicing, but the procedure becomes downright festive. Nobody dances in place and kicks up heels. It looks like yesterday and last week, except that the laughter sounds less strained. The staff and the surgeon have reason to feel useful and not helpless. To be on the job now justifies much other labor amid hopelessness. The cleaned end of the severed gut, clamped off half an inch back by duck-billed hemostats, is fat, roseate, like a baby's pout after feeding. Stearne praises a prompt surgical technician straightforwardly, saying, "She's good. She's very good," and even when he repeats the line every now and then until its meaning changes, he draws a chuckle or two.

As he jokes, he works, more gymnastically than he must during most operations. The surgical field is deep in the patient, diagonally in from the navel, between and below the iliac arch, and on down into the funnel of space inside the pelvic cradle. He sews with curved needles held in long-handled clamps. He is bent over, and under his gown, his hips rotate as he stitches, tests stitches, and stitches again. "She's very good." His voice echoes out of the damp abdomen. His surgical fields always end up looking splendid. A lattice of clamps suspends the site of his stitching in Fulleresque tension. "She's very good." He hands the severed foot of gut over to a nurse, for transportation to the pathology lab. He inserts a machine that looks like a caulking gun and is in fact a colon stapler into the patient's anus, from the outside, slides it up the stub of gut still extending inward, then slides the free end of the man's colon down onto the machine's tip from the inside, trims and tucks until all tissue is nicely placed, and then fires off a ring of stainless staples. Sealed, clean, cancer-free, the patient is again topologically identical to healthy persons, a torus, a doughnut, a solid with a hole through it, blood brother once more to every living thing further evolved than a paramecium. Into this patient, too, Stearne dumps a gallon of warm saline, as matter-of-factly as he

161

might fill up a washbasin. No bubbles. Job done. He closes quickly. He sutures the scar with monofiliment. He helps the very good technician undrape the patient. When he comes to the penis, he pauses and regards it. It's pointed chinward, taped, a catheter emerging from its tip.

"You want to see an example of passive aggression?" he asks.

He yanks the adhesive off the penis, perhaps more forcefully than is necessary.

"There," he says. "Now I don't have to go home and kick the dog."

———

Another week or two go by and I chat with Stearne by phone. I'm planning to write about my brief experience as a patient facing the prospect of having cancer. Could he tell me again what mild thing the laboratory report said I actually had, and how to spell it?

"What if I tell you I was lying and you have six months to live?" he asks.

Somewhere I realize even at this moment that the guarded man is chiding me for making much of a minor complaint—and at that, one that turned out to be even more minor than he'd predicted. But my will, so recently strengthened, to interpret his comments with due allowance for his rough trade once again deserts me. "First off," I answer, "I'd tell you that was a sadistic answer—then I'd ask you if it's true."

"It's not true. I wasn't lying. No cancer. You'll live a long time."

When I hang up I go hunting for the dog.

12

"I Think It's the Last Pain
You'll Have to Feel from This"

Surgeons cause pain. Whether or not they mean to do so—and of course most set their sights on the "fixing" and not on the hurting—has nothing to do with the fact of the pain their actions cause. The mere prospect of surgery makes those facing it think of mayhem, of the meticulous torture of saints favored by Renaissance painters. Heads worked over, one after another, noses entubed, mouths, too, stuffed with tubes and stifled under green cloth, gas fed in. Then down below, wrists strapped and impaled. Finally, bodies flensed with knives and worried with pincers, chisels, hammers, needles.

At some level of cognition, for both surgeon and patient, any operation in progress must retain its double meaning—of healing and of hurting. What is true of good poets—that they acknowledge and work with all stray meanings of all that they do—is decidedly not true of surgeons. Surgeons veil from themselves emotion-laden aspects of what they do. But in half-known ways, they must traffic not just in the noble emotions but also in the guilty ones; they must feel heroic and sensible and kindly, but also naughty, and superior, and even afraid.

The aftermath of my hip surgery, many years ago, was pain. I cannot quite recreate the sensation; no cataclysm since has come close—not when I tumbled down a hill, hammered a finger, or suffered a nasty bite from my friend Angelo Mazzei's dog. After that surgery, the pain possessed me for three days. The presence of pain became my first and strongest postsurgical association, and the main evidence that I was still alive. The surgeon did visit once or twice and prescribed painkiller that helped some. But I knew: the surgeon—he's the one who done it to me.

He must have known, and cared routinely about how I felt. I was healing. He'd given me appropriate treatment. He'd done what he could. I've now witnessed the plights of dozens of patients the day after surgery, and it would have been maudlin and pointless for any surgeon to have spent much empathy on their sensations of pain. Postsurgically, patients hurt and they heal. It nearly always happens that way. Andersson, Stearne, and my old hip surgeon all thought about the fact, if not the sensation, of pain regularly. Patients feel the pain surgeons cause. For patients, though, pain is not fact but invasive presence, occupation. Strong pain changes everything.

———————◆———————

"I've been here before," an old man whispers with alarm. He is rolled slowly into the angiography room in Andersson's hospital, and set in place directly under a huge overhead X-ray machine. He fills the cart. His head has been capped in a green paper throwaway. He has a square, jowly face and hyperthyroid eyes that stare dolefully up at the machines that have come into his view. "I've been here in '69, '70, '72, '78, '80 . . ." His voice fades away.

Andersson and two nurses shuffle things about on the tool tables that surround the patient, assembling a disposable kit they will use to shoot radio-opaque dye into the patient's aorta.

"This won't take too long, Mr. D'Assay," says Doreen, over her shoulder. He stares upward. Packages are torn near his ears, making sharp ripping sounds; tubes rattle and plungers slither into them; blades and handles snap together with the click of self-locking joints.

The X-ray technician, wiry and thin, moves like a sailor in a strong wind. With abrupt, chopped-off gestures, she ties a yellowed apron—oilcloth on lead—around Andersson. She passes aprons to the nurses and to me.

She trots to the X-ray machine, grabs its bicycle grips, like a submarine pilot in a World War II movie maneuvering the periscope. She flips on a sighting lamp that shoots out an orange square, quartered by a shadow cross, against the bridge of Mr. D'Assay's nose. "I do not like this," he says, squinting. "I have been through this many times."

With a hollow needle the size of a soda straw, Andersson penetrates the right side of the neck. D'Assay stares straight toward the light, with the grim intensity of those escaping into consciousness only of the moment. This should take only a few minutes. The patient is not anesthetized. Andersson works the spike intently, searching with its tip deep inside the neck. He probes with little stirring motions. It's routine at first. But he's still probing after five awful minutes, and his eyes pierce toward the root of the needle as if they might see down through flesh to what he can't find. The search goes on for still another five minutes, by the clock. Finally, he stops trying. The patient closes staring eyes to rest, and moans, just once. Doreen abandons her battle station by Andersson's side and pets the patient's brow. "It won't be long now," she says softly into his ear.

Andersson turns the patient's head, and pushes the needle into the other side of the neck. D'Assay squints harder. This search works within a moment. Andersson finds the artery. In through the needle's hollow end he threads the tip of a thin, yard-long lead wire. It looks like a guitar string, like a pacemaker lead.

Andersson threads in lead, pinch by pinch. It wanders across the fluoroscope screen through the gray sea of organs, a black slash. It meets resistance. It won't thread in further. Andersson squeezes a squeeze bulb that he has fastened to the tail of the lead, and on the fluoroscope a dark little dot at the tip expands into a pale-white bubble; the wire slash floats upward, out of whatever cul-de-sac has caught it. He releases the bulb;

the pale balloon at the tip withdraws; the tip sinks, free. It's an elegant device. Andersson pinches in more wire. He steers the tip right and then left by his torquing of the free end. A rat in a video game circulatory maze, he feels his way all the way in.

Mr. D'Assay's face has iced into a fearful stare. Andersson takes in his patient's expression as he finishes threading in lead. "Almost done," he says with forced breeziness.

He connects a syringe now, in place of the squeeze bulb, and presses lightly on its plunger, several times. Small puffs of radio-opaque dye flow out of the tip on the screen, and marble with gray swirls that mark the turbulence of D'Assay's arterial blockage. Andersson nods. He has found out what he wished to know: where and how to operate. He draws out the long lead, and then, at last, its conduit of needle, from the neck.

D'Assay doesn't look relieved at all. His eyes squeeze shut completely. He won't talk. He's on strike. In a radio interview soon after Jacobo Timerman's *Prisoner Without a Name, Cell Without a Number* was published, the Argentinian editor offered what amounts to a hint for enduring torture: "If you remember the tenderness of your wife, you begin to need the tenderness of your wife. So you don't."

"Can you count backwards from ten, Mr. D'Assay?"

Nothing happens.

"There's some danger of a stroke following this procedure," Andersson says. Still nothing happens.

"Count to ten, sir!" Doreen urges him.

Still nothing. Something—perhaps it's not a stroke—has silenced Mr. D'Assay.

Finally, though, he does what he must to reassure Andersson. "Ten . . ." he says faintly. "Nine . . ."

———————

Scientists, social and physical, speak strangely of pain. To read Lawrence Kruger and Sandra Kroin's "Brief Historical Survey of Concepts in Pain Research," from Volume VIb of Academic Press's *Handbook of Perception*, one would suspect that suffering was some new oddity that had just been brought back like moon rocks:

> The uniqueness of pain in comparison with the other senses is that it may be associated with a subjective component of behavior—suffering—and that it appears to lack dependence upon a single sense. . . . The distinction between the sensation . . . and the . . . suffering . . . was not fully appreciated until modern times.

Congratulations to us moderns for separating wound from whimper! Dispassion is progress, and welcome after our long troglodytic millennia of fancying merely that what hurts hurts. Perhaps it's a philosophical side benefit of the age of anesthesia; nowadays, what hurts may not hurt.

A few anesthetics leave "sensation" more or less intact, but do in fact remove suffering. Nitrous oxide does it, and it was even briefly fashionable as a vaudeville exhibition in the 1840s. As the "me" generation knows, cocaine can do it too. There is also the opposite case. Patients under spinal anesthesia or nerve blocks feel no sensation, but do remain open to the psychological suffering of their experiences.

Pain (or is it suffering?) has been "described in several ways: with respect to quality (burning, stabbing, crushing); intensity (slight, moderate, severe); time course (brief, intermittent, continuous); location (superficial, deep, spreading), and so on," according to Richard Sternbach, in "Psychological Dimensions and Perceptual Analysis," in the same *Handbook of Perception.*

A functional cause of pain in all its varieties is suggested later in the *Handbook,* in Kenneth L. Casey's "Neural Mechanisms of Pain":

> The experience of unpleasantness requires a neural apparatus which ultimately motivates aversive behaviors, such as escape, or other somatic and autonomic responses. Pain, then, requires the participation of a neural system . . . subserving both a discriminative and a motivational function.

In the grandness of evolutionary logic, pain has proved essential to us. Its sensate articulateness suggests to the body where to slap the mosquito, how far and how fast to flee, where the spear is sticking in, which limb to limp upon while fleeing and nursing the wounds of a hard life, and when to go to and when to avoid surgeons. Pain provokes the body's appropriate participation in getting out of nasty jams. It's the latest news from the real world, and the impulse to react to the news, both built into each ache. It's the fittest's ticket to survival. The organism that has evolved from slime to sea slug to patient and surgeon has owed its success to pain the whole way along. Whoever can't hurt lacks the evolutionary pep to survive. The rhythm of evolution is tapped out in innumerable painful knocks suffered by a trillion creatures fleeing during a million years. Pain enables life; hurt embodies the miracle of our presence.

That pain is intermittent, therefore, seems as inevitable as its existence. If we hurt all the time, or never, how would one know when to run? Sternbach studied those few patients in medical literature—perhaps a score or so—who could not perceive pain. They have bitten off their tongues or fingers, and burned themselves regularly. Sternbach says that except in their deficient pain perception, they "were all described as normal . . . and those given extensive personality tests performed normally on them."

At the other extreme, patients with continuous, chronic pain seem among the most wretched of us. They may appear well, and so are frequently long treated by doctors as malingerers. Finally, they may end up with spinal or brain surgery for relief, and may consent to constant drugging, trading alertness for comfort.

C. S. Lewis, during the first days of World War II, by the gleam of a recently rekindled Christianity, in *The Problem of Pain* celebrates the intermittence of pain as a source of happiness. "Pain is not only immediately recognisable evil, but evil impossible to ignore, . . . pain insists on being attended to." When it is attended to, and its memory fades, the enduring consequence of pain is sweet: "When it is over, it is over, and the natural sequel is joy." Lewis concludes, "We are never safe, but we have plenty of fun, and some ecstasy."

———

Just a few days short of Christmas, in his cramped office, Andersson hands me a thin gift-wrapped box and wishes me "Happy holidays." I unwrap it. It's a maroon fountain pen, and a nice one. Coming from a man in a trade whose practices are tool-specific, in which the tool frequently defines the surgical procedure, the gift of a pen is hopeful. Perhaps with Andersson's pen I'll write Andersson's story. I try it. Very smooth. Works best at a slant. Skips occasionally. Never smears. Feeling like an ingrate, I thank him profusely.

"And another present," he says. "O'Rourke, room 218. A patient who can talk."

"What's he in for?" A question that would also suit a prison warden.

"I've got to do something for him. Replumb his leg, take it off—depends on what's in there."

"He can talk?"

"He's a journalist. This is unusual. Mine's a working-class practice. I think you'll like him."

"What kind of journalist? And what kind of disease?"

"I don't know what kind of journalist. He's said I can introduce you, and show you his chart." Andersson hands me a thick folder.

O'Rourke, Harry, had bladder cancer years ago. He had an ileostomy and voids urine into a sack. His new complaint is a cold and aching right foot. Yesterday, his arteriogram showed 40 percent occlusion of the right femoral artery. He's already had a left femoral-popliteal bypass. "Many vascular problems become bilateral, sooner or later," Andersson says, "and his has."

Upstairs, in the far window bed in 218, past three old men in three other beds, O'Rourke lies propped up, a *Reader's Di-*

169

gest gripped in one big paw. He's a hearty, smiling man with pale, blotchy skin and short white hair. He shakes the little magazine. "I'm facing the same sort of procedure that's written about in this latest issue. This gives me hope." His shaggy white eyebrows curl up at the ends when he smiles. Hope turns out to be a much-practiced discipline for him, one that has brought him through a hard life. He wants to talk. I scarcely have a chance to frame questions. He knows what's on his mind, and speaks with a sense of urgency.

"The subject in question is the body of O'Rourke. It has some pain now, but my background has conditioned me for thinking about the animal in trouble. I was a police reporter—for the New York *American,* later the *Journal-American.* It was in the thirties. There were seven murders that winter. The average take was sixteen dollars each. The price of life wasn't much more than what they used to say it was in the Orient.

"Then I was in the Pacific, in the marines, in the war. I made five assault landings as a marine. Death got common. My criticism was that it was so undignified. A guy sprawled out with a mouthful of sand. That's all. In more organized form, it's what a lot of people saw when TV brought Vietnam into their living rooms. Of course, knowing the people made a difference.

"The old Chevalier line, 'You've got to consider the alternatives'—it gets to me. I'm down for eight A.M. tomorrow. The well-being of O'Rourke, I've given it a lot of thought. Tennis, athletics—I used to be very active. I cut wood. I gardened, a fifty-by-hundred-foot garden every year, year after year.

"What they have to do should take three to five hours. I had five weeks of thinking I had a pulled muscle. Then I called the GP and he said get right over to see Dr. Andersson. Dr. Andersson said he hated to put people in the hospital for Christmas. Here I am, so he must think there's a reason to be in a rush.

"Now I have a morbid curiosity—caused by the problem of suddenly changing from someone with a cold foot and aching calf to something more permanent. I said to Dr. Andersson, 'What's the worst case on this?' 'Amputating the leg,' he said. That shook me. I told him I didn't know if I preferred mutilation to death. One is terminal and the other is just getting off for a while at a way station, with serious loss encountered.

"At the arteriogram yesterday, I was very nervous. It was unpleasant. Now I've developed a more fatalistic attitude about tomorrow's surgery. If I went through this in my mind again and took these things for a walk, I'm not sure I'd come out in the same place. I might get nervous again. I would have accepted a terminal decision with more equanimity than an amputation.

"This machine's breaking down. It's been up and down a lot of roads. People think: It can't happen to me. My cousin got cancer years ago—I thought: Not me. Now that's happened to me twice. I had a malignancy of the larynx. One of the bladder two years later. I got past them. Now this. People ignore storm warnings. Those two boats lost in the storm in the Atlantic—it's in today's paper.

"Is there anything next? I wouldn't be surprised if there were an afterlife. Oh—no seven ranks of angels. No Golden Gates of Peter, hand on the throttle. Articles giving positions on the Virgin Birth are unimportant. If there'd been a natural conception, and *then* a birth of a miraculous being—even that would have been a hard thing to do."

At the end of the second-floor corridor of the hospital, on a shelf above the nurses' station, the staff has assembled a crèche—doll's cradle with ceramic holy baby, toy trees, and a Lincoln-log shed streaked with spray snow and strewn with aluminum tinsel. As I pass, the nurses' radio carols thinly, an Irish-whiskey tenor in the midst of "Good King Wenceslas":

Page and monarch, forth they went,
Forth they went together,
Through the wild winds' rude lament,
And the bitter weather.

———————

Coincidentally, I see O'Rourke again just a few days past Easter. He is up and out of bed and returned to his farm in

171

rugged New England hills. He walks slowly to greet me, showing only the slightest leftward limp. He winces as he steps off his
patio, and he waves his arm out over a broad view of mountains
that have just begun greening with new leaves. He puts his hand
on my shoulder.

"An artist told me he could see eleven shades of green
here," he says. "Highest mountain in the state is two degrees
east of that bump there." He smiles with satisfaction. It's a beautiful spring day, one of the first of the year. He throws up both
hands. "Hell, this is the last time I'll live, and I might as well do
it right," he says. He's stored away his earlier manic absorption
in his plight. He concentrates instead on the green hillside. I
remark that his surgery has worked—and he still has his leg. He
takes up the topic reluctantly:

"Your memory tends to paper these things over. There's
very little future in retrospect. Like my generation, I tend to be
fatalistic." He settles me down in a deep-dish wing chair across
from him on the patio, feeds me potato chips and beer, and then
obligingly tries to steam off some of the papering over. But his
recollection is merciful to him; it has improved on events.

"Before the operation," he says, "I felt no apprehension
that registered. I kind of wondered in bed what the outcome
would be. I was parked outside the operating room for a while,
just before the surgery—no, maybe that was before another operation. Anyway, an orderly drew up with a cart of tools. I
looked over and I could see that just about everything I had on
my workbench at home was there. I thought, at that moment:
For my generation, continual life with vitality is a race with
medical advance.

"After the operation I was scarcely aware. You hear con-
versations, but they don't register on the blackboard. Then, over
in intensive care, I slowly came out of it. A relaxed period. I
napped a lot. I regained consciousness in depth—not just the
ability to see and hear. I woke up and I felt the bed was at a
forty-five-degree angle. I knew it wasn't true. Daily, things got
better.

"Dr. Andersson drew an 'X' with a Magic Marker on my

foot so the nurses could find the pulses easily. There was one gal who was a love, an attractive woman, forty-five or so. A couple of the other nurses were attractive and recently married. They kidded me about my cold feet.

"Dr. Andersson came in and said he was delighted. Of course, you know he's always saying things like 'super'—it's his favorite adjective. I said to myself, If it's that good, why examine the gift horse's mouth? You quickly forget how intense pain can be. I saw a friend once who'd just had a hemorrhoidectomy. I said to him, 'How do you feel?' He said, 'So bad I'd jump out the window, but I'm afraid I'd fall on my ass.'

"Now the pain's gone and I feel great relief. And it didn't cost much because of Medicare, and the insurance company. They paid about six thousand. Dr. Andersson charged about nine hundred, for three hours of surgery. He must feel as if he's playing God, invading the body like that."

"Did you feel," I asked O'Rourke, "that he was invading *your* body?"

"I had no feeling of it."

Andersson does not speak directly to the question of his postsurgical effects on patients. "He's still got rusty pipes, but he's got lots more mileage in him," sums up his involvement with O'Rourke—no further revelation on his part that he is personally tangled up with O'Rourke's passion of suffering, survival, and renewal. Pain separates patient from surgeon, placing them in distant and self-absorbing worlds, the one of fear, the other of guarded technical questioning: "Which tools?" and "How to?" and "Am I doing it well?"

There's a small psychological literature of works such as *The Psychodynamics of Surgical Practice*, by James Titchener and Maurice Levine. These books seem never to deal with *surgeons'* psychology, but always with patients'. Titchener and Levine do shed some light on O'Rourke's presurgical intensity: "Faced with loss of parts of the body, people are psychologically

173

impelled toward narcissism and withdrawal."

And they help explain his postsurgical rosiness; they offer a list of five common defenses against the overwhelming experience of having had surgery:

1. busyness
2. playing the role of the sweetest patient ever
3. displacement—i.e., "The food around here is awful"
4. projection—i.e., "Everyone seems down on me here"
5. passivity—i.e., "I wouldn't hurt a soul"

O'Rourke had concentrated, with very mellow results, on numbers 1, 2, and 5. After my hip surgery, numbers 3 and 4 sustained me, far less pleasantly. The authors suggest that all these methods minimize subconsciously anticipated punishment. They say that many patients feel that having accepted surgery was suicidal—moving toward and not away from pain—and also that, finding themselves alive, patients feel obliged to act intensely grateful to their surgeons.

O'Rourke, after handing me a second beer, gazes at the eleven spring shades in his mountain view, then says, reflectively, "I'm sure the medical profession is a long way from curing what I've got. But I'm also sure that there are many talented and selfless people working on it. And the hospital people—they were caring, friendly, supportive. There was practically *too* much attention. And if Dr. Andersson has developed a little bit of a macho image—it can be justified." We sit in silence. Wind on the new leaves makes the green view shimmer. O'Rourke says, "For the last three months I've been studying the recorder. I play little tunes. 'Tabor,' and 'Silent, Silent,' and 'My Little Boat.'"

———————

A sociologist, Mark Zborowski, once found that the meaning patients attach to pain has something to do with their ethnic backgrounds. Italians seemed "mostly concerned with the immediacy of their sensation rather than with its future effects or its symptomatic significance," he wrote in *People in Pain*.

Jewish patients "tended to describe their pain mostly as very severe . . . they tended to express their pain by groaning and moaning . . . in their anxiety about the cause and future implications of the pain . . . were concerned with finding the most skillful physician."

The Irish "tended to be rather helpless in explaining their illness and were prone to seek the cause within themselves. This helplessness as well as a resigned attitude toward the impact of illness seemed to be reflected in their passive and uncomplaining role as patients."

"The Old American appeared to be unemotional and to be trying to play down his suffering. When in pain he tended to withdraw. . . . Old Americans tended to leave it all to the physician."

I had indeed hurt Jewishly after my hip operation, whole-heartedly, socially, and in full dread of the meaning of symptoms. And O'Rourke, in the aftermath of his leg surgery, seems to have defied Zborowski's ideal types. He had complained like an Italian, worried like a Jew, felt as overwrought as an Irishman, and suffered most of his ordeal stoically enough to please a whole staff of Yankee nurses.

Russell Stearne takes shifts as general surgeon on call in his hospital's emergency room, and so sees many patients whose discomfort is not of his making, and for whom he represents succor and not torment. "Does it make me feel good to stop people from hurting? I suppose so," he says, as if he's never thought of it before. Late one afternoon, he's called in to attend to a young "Old American" who has had a nasty accident. He finds a spare, wiry boy of about nineteen in an alcove off the large emergency room, perched on a black stool. Nurses have trimmed away the left leg of the boy's blood-spattered blue jeans. He has tight curls of red hair and a fine-boned face, balanced above a huge Adam's apple. His thin neck is bent and he stares down at his thigh, at an oval gash in it six inches long. He must have injured it a while ago; there's no more bleeding, just fuchsia sloping walls ringing a level floor of exposed muscle, a bas-relief of shark's mouth carved in wiry leg.

In spite of his obvious discomfort, when a nurse says, "This is Dr. Stearne," he rises politely and automatically from the stool, balanced on his good leg, offers a shy smile, and introduces himself. "Gene Clampers," he says. He nods slightly, actually makes a small bow, before sitting again.

I have heard about the Clampers family before—they are a regional legend for their backwoods industriousness. A network of Clampers cousins and uncles conducts a prosperous logging trade. The boy has cut himself with a chainsaw. "Most of the chainsaw accidents that happen to professional loggers happen about this time of day—you get tired but it's not quitting time yet," Stearne tells him. He nods again. Such accidents run in the large Clampers family.

A logger, Dick Mayer, once had described a noon dinner in the Clampers farmhouse. He had brought down a load of logs and had been invited to stay. There were old Mr. Clampers, his wife—who cooked for the crew every day—and seven boys. Grandma Clampers served, finally seated herself, and called for grace. "I peeked during that grace," Dick Mayer had recalled. "I looked at one pair of hands and then at the next. I couldn't help counting up fingers. You know, not a person there, save for Mrs. Clampers and me, had ten fingers. Most of them had nine, and a few had eight or seven."

The current Clampers generation seems to be moving from fingers to legs. Gene Clampers is clearly miserable, yet he sits quietly, with a strained, straight face. A stocky cousin, not much past sixteen, who has brought the patient in, and whose own blue jeans are bloody too, hovers attentively, and helps Gene Clampers limp from the stool to a pipe-framed examining table.

"I'm working on with the family just until the end of the month to pick up a little cash," says Clampers to distract himself. "Then I'm signed up in the navy. I want to be a fighter pilot." Stearne wriggles his hands into rubber surgical gloves and prods four fingers down, right next to the wound on clean

176

flesh. The boy winces. Physiologists explain that when a person's skin is torn, the pain receptors in the area become more sensitive: a light touch or a drop of water that normally would seem incidental becomes excruciating.

A nurse prepares solace, sucking novocaine from a tipped bottle into a fat syringe. Stearne pierces the wall of the wound and injects a small share of the anesthetic, then pierces it again a few millimeters along the edge of the cut. He circumnavigates, injects, moves, and jabs again, circling the wound. As Stearne injects, young Clampers grips the pipes on the sides of the examining table so hard that each muscle in his long arms articulates. Plump veins rise out of his biceps and tears flow out of his eyes. He stays quiet. Relief comes on slowly. A minute passes, and finally he realizes he's become numbed, safe now, not in for more of the same. He breathes. He looks ashamed.

His cousin, watching closely, grows embarrassed. He clears his throat, laughs nervously a few times, and says, "Boy, Gene, we should have had a strength meter on that bench while you were pulling on it." Gene smiles.

Stearne cleans and neatens the injury. He draws its dulled sides together with large black stitches, then draws the skin together, laying down a neat track of smaller stitches above the deeper row. When he's done, the wound is gone, a shark that's dived back down.

———————

There's more of the same for Stearne. Clampers leaves, waving goodbye, clowning with his cousin, limping. A young emergency room doctor comes up to Stearne and says, under his breath, "I'm going to do you a favor by warning you that the next guy we've got for you—old guy with a mauled hand—his wife's angry as can be. She doesn't like it *at all* that they had to wait for the surgeon."

Stearne takes this new patient's chart. It seems the patient has indeed been waiting—an hour and fifteen minutes here; it's half-past five. And before arriving, he had spent a while at the

HMO a few towns away. His hand has been crushed since mid-afternoon, when he snagged it in the spiraling auger of a snow-blower. "Thanks for the warning," Stearne says.

But when he walks to the back of the treatment room and says hello to the old man, he is greeted affably in return, and that's that. The man has a square face, made squarer still by a trim white beard. His wife holds his right hand. She smiles at the doctor. Her husband's left hand rests on a pillow, and the pillow rests on his chest. He's lying on a litter. Stearne asks, as he gently unwraps the towels protecting the hand, "Are you in pain?"

"It is rather strong," the man says, conversationally, with an elegant Boston accent.

Stearne orders painkiller, and a hefty, gray-haired nurse, hovering, has the medication injected into the man's good arm within moments, as if she's been awaiting the chance. The patient allows that he was foolish—trying to clear a snagged branch from a running machine. The gray-haired nurse disappears—shift change, perhaps—and a taller, very pale replacement is suddenly standing there instead. The new nurse's eyes, sunken below strong brows, are so light a blue they seem nearly white. And upon her moon-round face a smile, a matter of set policy rather than of responsiveness, sits installed. She wheels the patient's bed into a treatment room, leaving the secretly angry wife behind. Now the smiling nurse touches the patient, strokes his shoulder, and keeps doing so for the next half hour without altering expression.

It becomes clear that except around snowblowers, this old man can take care of himself. He ignores wound and setting and speaks of the college (a very good college) where "I taught for years, chaired the history department, was even president for a while. I went away to Washington for a time and was an under secretary of state." He names names, tells stories about old royalty now retired to the hills around town. He's vital. Neither pain nor injury dulls his vivacity.

Stearne and the nurse set a cloth screen so the man can't watch what's about to happen down at the fingers. Stearne inspects the damage. The hand is mauled. The machine has torn away the tips of three fingers, and left the end of each a red smudge of bone, skin, and shredded nail. Stearne lays out the hand, palm up, upon a worktable, and starts organizing. He says little about the man's condition, how he sizes it up, what he intends to do—just, "I'm going to fix this up. It may hurt while I put anesthetic in it." For the second time in an hour, he begins injecting novocaine. The needle is so fat the blackness of its hollow core shows clearly. The patient suddenly ceases reminiscing and frowns more at each successive assault. The needle tours the thumb side of each torn finger, and then, refilled from a second bottle of anesthetic, tours the off side of the same fingers.

"That pain is the needle," murmurs the moon-faced nurse, stroking him, "but it's about over, and I think it's the last pain you'll have to feel from this." In general, my blueblood pals hate casual touching, but the old man seems grateful as he nods his understanding. I myself like comforting, the more the better, in sickness and in health.

The final needle slides in and out, at last without registering on the man's face. He takes up our interrupted conversation, speaking out strongly against Reagan's arms budget. Stearne still likes Reagan. He offers no opinions as he works.

He trims ribbons of stray flesh with scalpel and scissors, deftly, creating neat, vascularized cylindrical rims around finger stubs. He smooths the roughness of the stubs. He takes a dreadful tool called a rongeur, a nippers whose bite is levered by handles hinged like a scissors jack, and pinches away mushrooms of raw white bone that protrude above the neatened fingertips.

"I play the guitar. Have since nineteen twenty-four."

"You will again. You're only losing half an inch from these fingers."

Stearne, on the far side of the cloth screen, launches without warning into a very peculiar story. It seems to me more a hospital folk tale than something that could have happened, but it wanders into Stearne's mind and he vouches for it: "I heard

179

this the other day from a nurse whose friend in upstate New York was the one involved. At least so she said. It seems this woman, who was also a nurse and lives alone, came home from work, opened the door, and found her pet Doberman pinscher choking to death in the front hall." Stearne, needle in hand, glances over and assures himself the old man is listening. "She couldn't understand it, but she picked the dog up, lugged him to the car, and drove him down the street to the vet's. The vet took the dog into the back, then came out a few minutes later and told the woman her dog was now O.K., but that what he'd found in the dog's throat made him say she shouldn't go home. She should call the police and have them go to her house. The dog had been choking on four large black human fingers. The police were called, and when they searched the house, they found a black man, dead, where he'd crawled under the bed upstairs. He'd bled out."

"I didn't bleed much," the old man says from across the low screen.

"No, the vessels go into spasm and close off to save blood, except in massive injuries. But that story could have happened, medically," Stearne says.

Meanwhile, he has sealed each finger stump with fine, even stitching, crimping cupped flesh over the lost tips. When he's done, the fingers look like the rolled bottoms of half-spent toothpaste tubes. The old man eases himself up with a grunt.

In the waiting room, Stearne finds the man's wife. She's a decade younger than her husband, and wears enormous high-fashion glasses that magnify arches of brow above a broad, leathery smile.

"He's fine. It could have been much worse. You can take him home," says Stearne.

"He's a special man. I'm constantly amazed by his resourcefulness," the wife says.

Stearne tells the man, "You'll be all right now. Make an appointment to see me again in a few days. And the nurse will give you something to take if you're in pain later."

Stearne finds his coat, and heading home, passes the young emergency room doctor again.

"How did it go?" the young man asks.

"They weren't mad at me," Stearne says. "It doesn't pay to get angry at your surgeon."

13

"There Is No Gatekeeper
on Surgical Quality"

Everyone's angry with surgeons, and at dimmer targets the surgeons only represent—death, pain, expense, disruption, power, class, accomplishment, membership in a secret club. Most everyone also tends to love this or that surgeon in particular—everyone's own was the best in town. And both attitudes stand to reason. Surgeons not only heal the sick and wounded, they also make money doing it. Surgeons help out, but are in business. They profit as best they can from our needfulness, and they protect their opportunities for profitmaking, as other business people do. "I feel like a fight bull, with the picadors riding around sticking things into me," Andersson has said more than once. He likes to say it.

He finds his right to make a handsome living constantly and unjustly threatened. He feels that he does what he does well, under emotionally trying conditions, fending off patients' wishful desires to be safe, while "doing all I can do to make them comfortable for the duration." His colleagues will chide him if he very often undertakes precipitous or nonstandard actions. Patients will sue him if he neglects crucial details of their treatments, or even appears to do so. Andersson had one narrow escape from a lawsuit. He recalls his relief: "It's a cliché, but I really did it once, when I was young, years back—I left a sponge in a patient. It's easy enough to do. Every surgeon comes close once in a while; now I have tighter routines. Everything is counted going in and coming out—before I close up. But that time, once I realized the trouble, I just told the patient. He was understanding, fortunately. We reoperated and removed it and that was that. No harmful effects. I've gotten cautious, and it extends to other things. Tests—I order some I don't feel I need, just because of legal pressure to do everything. It doesn't always work best for the patient who has to endure the tests, and it's expensive for whoever's paying the bill. But I'm not going to open my tail up to any suit. I ask for the tests—and I count sponges."

Andersson feels *embattled*—and it seems to be an emotion shared by most surgeons I encounter. Patients' expectations, peers' scrutiny, legal threats, operating in proximity to death and pain, and at the limits of how much one can actually help—each takes its toll. The result seems almost inevitably to be that after some years of practice, surgeons slip into a kind of discipline-wide seclusion, the seclusion of morticians, or moguls, or famous actors; none of them wish to give up what they do well and profitably, but they come to find socializing with outsiders burdensome.

Andersson minds his manners, and proceeds cautiously with patients and medical peers. He holds visions of mortality at bay, and has a self-mocking cast to his occasional jokes.

Patients' criticisms, when they reach him, he must often take as evidence of their illness or ingratitude, although fawning gratitude is more often the side of their feelings they show him. Once he told me that a hostile patient didn't mean to be that way, but that she had suffered damage as a result of her illness. Attacks by medical reformers rarely reach him; he commutes, enclosed by his mission, from hospital to hospital, operating room to operating room, and resort to summer home, and rarely finds himself on unfamiliar ground. He knows that people out there say medical care is overpriced, may be inappropriately offered or withheld, is too passive, fragmented, and too rarely preventive, and he knows that surgeons in particular are said to be cold and overeager. But such criticism glances off Andersson's embattled consciousness. He contents himself with feeling he does "the best job I can to give quality care." He keeps coming back to the motif that he's the "mother hen." And in his terms it is true; he is obviously caring, he's infallibly considerate, and he takes trouble with those who come to be his patients.

The threats to his livelihood and good self-image that come from his medical peers do not simply glance off. They cut deep and make him cautious. The alliance of common interest among doctors long precedes the AMA. And while doctors habitually keep one another informed about colleagues' failings and eccentricities, they close ranks against outsiders, publicly construing cases of questionable practices in the best possible light, deflecting criticism by invoking fact and their shared expertise. There is some justice in this stance. Sick bodies' signals can be ambiguous and elusive. Even in the clearest of cases, where classic clinical signs call for a particular operation, and where the failure to go ahead with it would in itself constitute malpractice, surgeons may occasionally go ahead, only to encounter surprises.

Much—even most—of surgical diagnosis is not certain, but merely quite probable. Many disease processes are progressive, especially in the areas of cancer and vascular illness which Stearne and Andersson deal with. The efficacy of some surgical procedures is equivocal. And the eternal hot debate, the one that replicates in ideology the administrative separation of surgeons and internists, is the debate about when in the course of an advancing disease to intervene with a scalpel. When does the benefit of a surgical procedure outweigh its suffering and risk, and the usefulness of prolonging noninvasive treatment? Surgeons, say internists, are unsubtle, overeager, and poor diagnosticians. Internists, say surgeons, loiter, and confound clear enough indications with unwieldy erudition and undue hesitation.

Even within the ranks of surgeons, on any procedure there is likely to be a range of opinion on when it's right to intervene. In the past decade, tonsillectomies have dropped from the top, right down off the list of ten most common operations, as the consensus on the appropriate threshold for surgical intervention has shifted upward. The shift didn't happen dispassionately, by calm vote of "scientists," but represents research evidence slowly overtaking clinical theory, long habit, and private advantage. No doubt the shift was accompanied by a million instances of scorn, backbiting, gossip, confrontation, mostly out of public sight. Surgical progress seems generally to be an adversarial proceeding.

In the very current debate about when, in the progression of vascular disease, a surgeon ought to perform a carotid endarterectomy, Andersson describes himself as "an activist." He's convinced the carotid endarterectomy restores cerebral function and reduces risk of stroke for patients of his whose carotid arteries are closing with atherosclerotic plaque—usually old patients, and usually patients with other things also wrong with them. The procedure is moderately demanding, for both anesthesiologist and surgeon. Not all surgeons undertake it. It takes anatomical sophistication to navigate through the close, crucial structures of the neck. The small diameter of the carotid calls for delicacy in clearing obstructions and in stitching. Regulating the patients' vital functions during surgery is especially challenging.

Carotid endarterectomies carry relatively high risks—1 to 5 percent of patients die or suffer strokes as a result of the surgery. Surgical journals have, for the past few years, carried on a continuing evidentiary debate about when to intervene. Some surgeons won't perform the procedure unless, in addition to all other symptoms, patients have experienced transient ischemic attacks—TIAs—the small temporary stroke whose symptoms include dizziness, perception of flashing light, narrowing of the visual field, blacking out.

Andersson and many other vascular surgeons argue that by the time patients experience these TIAs, they are likely to be so sick that the risk of operating on them is far higher than it might have been a month or a year earlier, when the same inevitable disease process was already under way. Andersson favors operating when the indications are merely high blood pressure, pronounced bruit sounds (the sounds of blood pulsing past arterial constriction), and X-ray evidence of severe blockage. If these symptoms are present, he recommends operating even if patients are otherwise healthy.

A debate such as this—and it is only one of hundreds current about appropriate protocols for surgical procedures—represents the nature of progress in surgery. This is in one sense a scientific problem, resolvable in general, at least, as research results come in, and as refinements of operating procedure further lower risk.

But as long as the debate continues, attitudes about it, in hospital corridors and in annals of surgery, are not clean and emotionless science. Adherents to both sides become righteous ideologues. And Andersson's position as an "activist" makes him politically vulnerable to in-house charges of trendiness, profit-making, and precipitousness leveled by older, more conservative practitioners. If his chief of surgery, or members of the hospital tissue committee, or local powers active in professional subspecialist groups, turn out to disapprove of Andersson's style of intervention, Andersson will be affected by their judgment. Their word can curtail the flow of referrals that keeps him prosperous. Raised eyebrows lower income. It's a political process that seems inherently biased toward conservative medicine. It keeps youngsters in line, and medical progress advancing stolidly. While this may slow impetuous surgeons given to rescue fantasies, it may also inhibit the autonomous exercise of options that make sense in particular cases but are politically inexpedient for the surgeon. The better a surgeon's standing in the world of surgical power politics, the freer he may feel to stand apart from common practice when he sees fit. Being successful as a surgeon calls for political astuteness as well as manual dexterity.

————

Surgeons do business every time they operate, and their business comes to them largely from other doctors who think well of them. Surgeons are, in that sense, doctors' doctors, and their clients are not just the patients they repair but also the doctors who send the patients. In this way, too, being successful as a surgeon has as much to do with diplomacy within the medical community as it does with surgical skill.

At the end of one long workday, following upon a string of similar days, with Culver on holiday and the elders of the practice out of the picture, Stearne tiredly reflects. He sighs as he sits in his easy chair, legs akimbo. He's performed three operations and seen a score of patients, then handled two more patients in the emergency room. He breathes in the quiet of the darkening office for a while, and then, smiling at his own perversity, says, "You know, I wish there were more patients out there for me to see. I like to be tired from too much work."

"How could you get more?"

"Certainly not from the yellow pages—I just paid their bill and I don't know why I bother. Nobody calls *me* from that listing. Dr. *Stearne*. It's forbidding. People look in the local book and they call Dr. Goode, Dr. Smiley, Dr. St. James.

"In medical school they told us you've got to know about how bodies work. They taught us that. All they ever said about the business side of things is that you have to know the three A's, and that, they say, can't be taught. Affability, Availability, and Ability—and in that order."

"How do you rate yourself on them?"

"Ability—I'm very good. Availability—I'm a worker. I do pretty well there. Affability? I'm like most surgeons. I'm not too damned affable. I'm quick to tell people off. It hurts me. I used to say anything I wanted to when I first started practice. I've cut that out. It hurts me. Still, one of our older partners said, at his retirement party, that the biggest mystery for him remains why another doctor refers patients to you, and when, and how. It has no coherent pattern to it. It starts and stops without apparent reason."

The average general surgeon in the United States, according to one study, spends about twenty-two hours a week in office visits with seventy-four patients. Surprisingly, almost half of them are self-referrals—patients who do look in the yellow pages or who have listened to friends' recommendations. A third of referrals come from other physicians.

On the basis, frequently, of single visits, general surgeons tend to refer about one in five patients onward to other surgeons. Most visits to surgeons' offices aren't initial consultations, but sequels for discussing findings, for further evaluation, or for postoperative follow-up. About half of those who do come to visit general surgeons end up on their operating tables.

For all that, most surgeons, including Stearne (but not Andersson), don't work as much as they might. The nation's board-certified surgeons (who have met certification requirements of various specialties' Boards of Surgery) do between 75 and 90 percent of the nation's surgery, depending on the sort of operation. A third of general surgeons do at least an operation every other day, and another third, more than two hundred a year.

The supply of surgeons seems adequate for current demand. The problems are not in number but in distribution—poor and rural areas get shortchanged. Blacks, for example, are from 220 to 330 percent more likely than whites to end up under the care of surgeons still in training (depending on the procedure). And the cancers of black patients, when first discovered, are more advanced and therefore less curable—perhaps in part because surgeons are less accessible to blacks.

By controlling size of the population of surgeons, current practitioners can limit to some extent their impending competition. A government study in 1980 projected an oversupply of physicians, including surgeons. Curiously, the American College of Surgeons' official response to this projection was rather laissez-faire—they opposed reductions in training programs. They argued that one can't anticipate what future technology may make possible. At the moment, there are plenty of surgeons, and enough work so that it's unlikely any need be impoverished.

By the laws of economics, one might guess that this plenitude would set surgeon against surgeon, and bid down the price of every appendectomy. Of course, things don't work that way. Some studies have shown that demand for surgery increases as supply of surgeons increases—bring a new surgeon to town, and he'll find patients to work on, without appreciably draining other surgeons' practices. Also, patients rarely ask about price, rarely comparison shop, and rarely even seek second opinions before accepting their surgeons' advice. Patients go, and trust.

When second opinions are required by insurance plans, nearly a fifth of them, according to some research, fail to confirm initial recommendations. But patients once in pursuit of cure seem either to grow eager for surgery, or else to be eagerly directed by advisers; about 70 percent of negative second opinions in one study got changed once again by *third* opinions. In the end, second opinions cause the rate of surgical intervention to decline only about 8 percent.

Not only don't patients shop around for price or question their surgeons' verdicts much, but patients also don't often select their surgeons on the basis of technical excellence. Stearne's patients, whenever I asked them, seemed to have chosen him on the basis of impressions built upon much trust and little knowledge. They looked him up—yes, in the yellow pages—and liked him when they met him. Or the HMO sent them over because he's the official HMO surgeon, so he must be pretty good. Or their family doctors sent them, saying he's supposed to be the best in town for this particular procedure. Or he saved a neighbor's life when the neighbor had something a few years ago. Or he took care of them when they were delivered to the emergency room, injured, so why switch now? "It has little coherent pattern to it," Stearne says. "I'm puzzled by it, but somehow they get here."

————◆————

Stearne is tired out by his long day. But a final emergency has come up, and it's a crucial one. No patient lies dying, while Stearne rushes back to the emergency room once again. And no one in intensive care, recovering from work Stearne's done on them this morning, has taken a turn for the worse. There's no patient. Stearne climbs into his Mercedes and rushes toward the hospital accounting office. A threatening phone call has interrupted his end-of-the-day reverie. It has come from the hospital's administrator, and what he's told Stearne is that per hospital regulation, approved with due process by the hospital board of trustees—no offense intended but rules are rules and this one has been ignored for too long, sir—Stearne may no longer schedule new surgical patients. At least not unless he shows up, completes, and signs his patients' backlogged charts. A stack of them a yard high has built up during the past month. And before patients' bills may be sent along to the government and insurance companies for collection, his signature must be on the documents. Come today, or forget about operating tomorrow. When Stearne parks in the hospital parking lot, it's already dark outside.

The power of this civilian authority to halt Stearne's lucrative trade even momentarily demonstrates one of the forces reshaping medicine. Surgeons, unlike the autonomous family doctors of a few decades ago, can't practice without hospitals. Hospitals store patients. They also store workshops and tools, and inventory supplies. They supply staffs of helpers. They supply seminars, libraries, and colleagues. And hospitals form alliances with other hospitals and with medical schools. Such alliances have become important contenders in the struggles among insurance companies, government regulators and payment agencies, the health products and drug industries, and professional medical interest groups. Hospitals house and schedule medical work. They supervise it. They provide business staff— much to the point in this case—who send out bills and collect money. In short, what hospital administrators do—the whole while limited in their authority by the collective autonomy and power of doctors—is to run bureaucratically large and politically complex businesses, and to protect their businesses' huge cash flow.

In not signing a month's worth of records, Stearne has tampered with that life's breath of hospitals. In days of twenty-percent money, administrators attempt extreme remedies.

It would be far more difficult for the hospital to suspend a surgeon's privileges for questionable medical practices than to

190

suspend them for messing with the business's cash flow. Stearne resignedly trudges through the hospital. The damp smell of meat gravy and instant mashed potatoes fills the corridors. As we ride the elevator upstairs, trolleys filled with domed plates ascend with us.

The accounting office has closed for the day. But Stearne's truant records—the stack is every inch of a yard high, recording in billable detail thirty-six hospital stays—has been left for him in the white-wallpapered workroom next to the medical library.

Stearne sets to work. He scans form after form, and signs on many dotted lines. The pile slowly lowers. As he works, he recites to me the month's inventory of cases, and he says how each patient came to seek his help.

1. Mrs. A., 66, foot pain from arterial stenosis, fem-pop bypass. Referred by John Smith, M.D. He's a very good doctor.

2. Mrs. B., 49, anal fissure—repaired. Marv Gold referred. One of the smart young internists. Refers me cases having to do with the digestive system. I don't know why.

3. Mr. C., 17, car accident. Broken teeth, saw him because I was on emergency room call when he came in.

4. Mr. D., 16, a kid from a local halfway house, prolapsed hemorrhoid. Another one from Gold.

5. Mr. E., 32, one of the Puerto Rican migrant workers who has stayed in the area. Umbilical hernia—repaired. His sister knows me somehow, he said.

6. Mrs. F., 86, stenosis—lack of blood—to hand, no surgery. Referred by Jay Locke—he has an office downstairs in my medical building.

7. Miss G., 57, colonic cyst—operated and removed. Called by the HMO—Dr. Williams over there, who sends me a lot of patients.

8. Mrs. H., 46, breast cancer—removed breast and two lymph nodes, and referred for further adjuvant chemotherapy. Another from the HMO, Dr. Doe.

9. Mrs. I., 24, sled accident, cut knee, repaired. Emergency room.

10. Mr. J., 62, right inguinal hernia. Used to see one of the older surgeons in my office.

11. Ms. K., 18, follicle cyst, and right lower quadrant pain. Fixed cyst, diagnosed gastroenteritis. University infirmary.

12. Mr. L., 51, aortic stenosis, performed aortic resection. He was a walk-in. I don't know why. Didn't ask.

13. Mr. M., 84, recurrent pneumothorax, right lower lobe, severe chronic lung disease, operated, patient died one week later, renal and cardiac failure.

14. Patient F. readmitted.

15. Patient N., 30, hernia, in and out, fixed, in one day. HMO.

16. Ms. O., 19, appendix, out in 2 days. University infirmary.

17. Ms. P., 40, infected knee, from a cow kick—there was manure in the wound. That came in through the HMO.

18. Mr. Q., 88, came in with gastric bleeding. No cancer found. Bleeding stopped, discharged. That came from Adams, an internist also in my building.

19. Mrs. R., 50, appendix. Through the emergency room.

20. Mr. S., 41, left upper quadrant pain after fall. Spleen was O.K. Observed and discharged next day. Through the emergency room.

21. Mr. T., 39, hernia. HMO.

22. Mrs. U., 82, bowel obstruction from adhesions resulting from previous surgery. Reoperated. She's an old patient of mine. I've operated on her for years.

23. Mrs. V., 29, cystitis, medicated. She's a hospital employee who stopped me in the hall.

24. Ms. W., 14, ingrown hair in gluteal cleft. Excised. University infirmary.

25. Mr. X., 40, hernia. I fixed it. He came in because I'd fixed his buddy's hernia.

26. Mr. Y., 86. He had pleural effusion, strial fibrillation, and congestive heart failure. Medicated. Discharged with a pulse of 72. I'd fixed his daughter for something or another.

27. Mr. Z., 35, hernia. A walk-in. No idea where he came from.

28. Mr. AA., 18, appendix. University infirmary.

29. Ms. BB., 25, rupture of some blood vessels in the corpus luteum, made surgical repair. Came in through the HMO.

30. Ms. CC., 30, cut up in an auto accident. University infirmary.

31. Mr. DD., 41, hernia. Out in three days. Uneventful. A walk-in. I'd treated him before for something or another.

32. Mrs. EE., diabetic with gangrenous foot. I did a fem-pop, and left her with a nice warm foot. She came in through John Smith, the internist. I helped bring him back to town.

33. Mrs. FF., cancer of the sigmoid colon. Operated. No evidence of distant spread. But metastases had occurred. Guarded prognosis. Dr. Doe, HMO.

34. Ms. GG., 19, horse fall. Left upper quadrant pain, did an examination for spleen injury. University infirmary.

35. Ms. HH., 55, hypercalcemia—recurrent kidney stones. Removed stones. I did her before, a hysterectomy. Another John Smith patient.

36. Mrs. EE. again. the 74-year-old diabetic with the fem-pop. Arterial insufficiency now, right foot. It threw emboli, clogged again. Rest pain. Fem-fem bypass.

Stearne signs his name a final time with a flourish of the felt-tip, and asks with a grin, "What do you make of all this? Where do they come from? I don't have that warmth and charm—but I'll bet I'm the busiest surgeon in the hospital."

The stack before him represents a fraction of his month's office patients, and a smaller fraction yet of the patients who continue to depend on him, off and on, for care of chronic ailments. Of the thirty-six admissions (including two readmissions) during the month, only seven came to him from private doctors. Five were walk-ins. Five were hand-me-downs from Stearne's retiring older partners. Four arrived after encountering him on his rotation in the hospital emergency room. And fourteen—nearly half his cases—came from the HMO whose work he does on contract, and from its subsidiary service at the university infirmary.

Of the seven new private referrals, two doctors sent him a single patient each. One doctor sent him two patients. And another, following a steady habit, referred three patients. This internist, John Smith, has a short and pleasant history with Stearne. Smith had left town for further training, but wished to set up nearby again. A local doctor had died, leaving an established practice, and Stearne thought to phone Smith cross-country, alerting him that an opportunity to return had appeared.

I sought out Dr. Smith and asked him about his methods of making surgical referrals. Smith is burly, brown-haired, and just at the moment of transition that befalls many successful men in their late thirties, when the edges round as athleticism gives way to gastronomy. He speaks in a low, confiding voice. "Stearne is one of two surgeons in the area I'd let operate on me for something serious," he says. "Two others I'd trust for bread-and-butter things—gall bladder, appendix. Why do I refer to Stearne? First of all, an internist never refers to someone he doesn't like and trust. I like and trust him. The next thing is, you first tell your patient, 'You need an operation, so do you have someone you want me to refer you to?' That's standard. Just about every patient who has had surgery before will then name the doctor who worked on them. Occasionally that will be someone I wouldn't send people to. So far, it's been for minor things, and the surgeons they named were adequate, so I didn't have to say anything.

"That leaves about seventy percent of my patients in need of surgery where, essentially, I'm the consumer. I'm the one choosing which surgeon to send the patient to. What do I do? I rotate, more or less, on the list of the four I've decided I especially trust. I make an effort to take personalities of patients and doctors into account, and also technical strengths of surgeons with regard to particular diseases. If I've sent a lot to one surgeon, I'll send some to another. My guess is that I send Dr.

Stearne about twenty patients a year. I don't keep track; I could be off by a hundred percent.

"Stearne has his peculiarities. Not everyone likes him. I happen to. Very much. And he's extremely technically competent. A little conservative about jumping in, say, on a patient he might think is too old, or too far gone, and he'll say, 'Well, it isn't worth doing this procedure.'

"Something else you have to bear in mind about surgeons— some are lucky. Just lucky. Two surgeons do everything right, and one gets better results. The other one's suture lines will separate, and he'll get infections or post-op complications. You can't put your finger on it, and say it's skill or judgment or care. Dr. Stearne is lucky. Some other surgeons around here are not. Dr. Goode is lucky. Dr. St. James is not. You see your patients over the years coming back to you. You hang out and you hear the nurses talking all over the hospital. You see other patients in the hospital, not just your own, and you hear talk about other cases too. Those are your sources. After a while, you get to know who is lucky."

This insistence by a man of science on the mysterious operation of luck seems inspired more by diplomacy than by the inscrutability of life. Having seen the same procedures repeated often and by different surgeons, I have come to suspect that "surgeon's luck" results from factors not closely associated with chance. Some surgeons are keener and better trained than others. They conceive sounder strategies. Beyond that are two traits that are virtually matters of character. One is mechanical finesse. Some surgeons—it takes only a few minutes of watching for even a layman to guess who they are—quite obviously are the kind of sound craftspeople who do all manual chores nicely. Stearne appears to be in this "lucky" club. The valentine cards its members made in fourth grade to bring home to mother no doubt arrived unwrinkled, and lacked any trace of white paste oozing between doily and backing.

The other telling aspect of "surgeon's luck" is consistency— day-upon-day and moment-after-moment, relentless, mood-proof consistency. Surgery frequently gets tedious. Details take hours to do right. They're the same details that took hours yesterday on someone else. Fixable mistakes get made, or step-by-step plans to do things routinely dissipate as unforeseeable interior conditions reveal themselves. Shoddy tissue turns up where sound stitching was expected, and an afternoon's work lengthens into evening. The "lucky" surgeons are the ones with patience and self-abnegation to go on composedly, still taking all the care they can. Such luck calls for a passionate interest in each job, and a detachment from such private concerns as having supper. Some surgeons I've watched have seemed in a constant contest to contain their own disorder. They scare the nurses.

I ask Dr. Smith if he has seen Stearne at work, if he in fact has had any occasion to judge his operating room technique, before putting him on the list of four trusted surgeons.

"No," he answers, "I've never seen him operate. And I wouldn't know what I was looking at if I did go in there, really. I haven't spent much time in an OR since medical school."

Then how, I ask him, can he form the judgment that Stearne is both lucky and "extremely technically competent"?

"I hear it—from operating room technicians, from nurses in the recovery room, from the staff in intensive care. Between us internists there's even a little hallway chat about surgeons— but in this city the internists don't get together much to chat about anything. You don't get much from the hospital committees that know what's going on—the tissue review committee, surgical mortality committee, the tumor board. Their procedures are confidential. It's true, some extreme situations do leak out, and there's a little information there.

"But now that I stop to think about it, I *do* actually feel fairly confident that I have had enough information to choose surgeons wisely for my patients. I have some of that information not from any official channels but because of—well, I might as well come out and say it—gossip, confidences of various sorts. I couldn't refer well without confidences I shouldn't officially have from nurses and from other physicians. It's easy to cut yourself out of that sort of thing too. Many doctors don't talk to

196

nurses. If you've got any sense, you keep your ear to the ground."

I go on the gossip trail, ear low. I eat lunches with Dr. Smith's secret sources. They don't see themselves that way. The first lunch is with a cheery anesthesiologist, who turns out to be unabashedly discreet. He has overseen anesthesia in thousands of operations—many of them performed by Stearne upon patients referred to him by Smith. One might anticipate that anesthesiologists, who are medically trained and on regular rotation with surgeons, expert witnesses to surgeons' every piece of work, would be the richest general source of news about operating room talent. One would suspect that family doctors would chat them up regularly on the subject. But it turns out that just as a surgeon sometimes calls the referring internist and not the patient his "client," so an anesthesiologist frequently comes to see the surgeon as a client. Anesthesiologists frequently see their jobs as requiring constant diplomacy, and they are obviously right—their work can make surgeons look good or careless, and in their daily presence they observe every minor mis-cut, every sloppiness before it gets corrected, every rash maneuver that works out, every display of fear and temper on the part of every surgeon. Every mistake. They know everyone's secrets and they acquire protective discretion.

"I may think to myself," the anesthesiologist tells me, "that some surgery is better than other surgery. But there are many gray areas in medicine—most everything is gray. If the medical community doesn't have allegiances to each other, what will happen? If surgeons feel too vulnerable they can't work well. And the public has to have faith in something. The staff down in surgery are like blood brothers.

"Now, if a GP or an internist comes right up to me—and it's happened all of three times in thirty years, even though I am, frankly, in a better position to know the best surgeons than most other doctors in the hospital—and asks me right out to rank the surgeons, I'll refuse. Then, if he's smart, he'll ask me next, 'Well, who's *your* surgeon?' That I will answer, and it's Dr. Stearne."

197

My next lunch is with a radiologist from the hospital. A genial, red-haired man in his fifties, he reads the X-rays—frequently before and after shots—of thousands of surgical patients a year, many of them Stearne's patients, including some referred along by Dr. Smith. Like the anesthesiologist, the radiologist is part of a partnership that is the hospital's main supplier of its sort of service. And like the anesthesiologist, the radiologist seems also in a good position—having both expertise, and access to evidence about almost every piece of surgery in the hospital—to guide referring physicians in making wise choices for their patients. He also sees himself as in the business of serving surgeons, just as much as patients, and he construes a *medical* rationale for keeping his inside knowledge of surgical quality to himself.

"I see enough information so I have very clear opinions of who I would like to have operate on me or my family, and who I wouldn't," he says. "Actually, the error rate in this hospital is incredibly low, compared to what I saw—gallstones missed on the first operation, and such—back when I was a resident.

"But of course, I do very occasionally see some problems. My group, doing all the radiology for the hospital, does not wish to lose our clients' confidence. If the surgeons can't be open with us, we can't help them. We provide a layer of quality control in recommending to surgeons the correct sequence of care. We can't be in a position to do that and also give out referral information too. We give a differential diagnosis of what something could be, and we suggest how to pursue it."

The radiologist says that the practice of medicine is so overshadowed by the threat of malpractice suits and by the egotism of certain practitioners he prefers not to name that even this layer of assistance must be offered in a special ironic tongue—a diction that will be understood by its expert readers to mean what it says strongly but that articulates it tentatively. "Our reports," the radiologist explains, "have to be done in a certain language; some physicians (rightly so, I'm sure) have feelings about that. They don't want us to be too specific in recommendations, because there may be medical-legal implications to our saying, 'This is what you *should* do.'

"Therefore, we give a list of suggestions as to what might possibly be done, 'if clinically indicated'—we frequently use that phrase to leave them free to do something else if they mean to. As a result, our satisfactions become intellectualized—whether or not we've been correct. Also, there's satisfaction in anticipating what things surgeons will need to know to work effectively."

I switch from lunches to breakfasts, and dine shortly after dawn with nurses and with surgical technicians. While they do not work under the discipline of a partnership of colleagues, the sole employer of their skills is the hospital in town. They all have seen Stearne work hundreds of times—including work he's done on Dr. Smith's patients, aided by the radiologist's deferential diagnoses and the discreet anesthesiologist's anesthesia—and they feel a need to be loyal to these friends and employers. They are aware of their replaceability in the hospital's scheme of things. Still, they have seen a lot, and they seem also to wish to be frank about what they know.

"GPs, especially the older ones, tend to refer most to surgeons with plastic personalities, and rely on those people rather than on details of surgery such as I see every day," one OR technician says. "No GP is going to walk up to a mere OR tech and ask, 'Hey, what do you think of so-and-so as a surgeon?' No. What they think is, 'We're the doctor and you're just the help.' It's too bad. They could get a lot of info. I've been doing this for better than ten years.

"As a matter of fact, most of the work I help out with seems pretty good—and believe me, when it's routine it is *boring* after all those years. I assist in four, five procedures a day, mostly, with different surgeons in each one sometimes, and I do that five days a week.

"But once in a while, a surgeon will be real jumpy, unsure of his anatomy—most often it's when they're trying to do something that's unusual for them, or something they haven't done in years. A simple operation can go bad. Things get tense then. Probably it will turn out O.K. anyway, and the patient will never know. But I have seen operations botched because of what I consider incompetency and lack of personal application.

"I do happen to be part of the OR team. It is hardly ever like that. Even when it is, I don't know if the surgeon is at fault or the *system* is at fault. Shouldn't there be rules? A surgeon should have to do a certain procedure each year in order to continue doing it, for example."

Another operating room regular, a sturdy and very tall nurse who has scrubbed in daily for half a dozen years, speaks, at another breakfast, with similar bewilderment and frustration about her judgments of surgeons. "I may think," she says, "that the operation is not going as well as it should, and I may think the problem is the surgeon is not as skilled as some others. But who am I to say? Alone, off by ourselves, we'll call them names. We'll make gross jokes about them afterwards. But actually we're so busy—there's always a next operation to set up for. We're pretty tight, though, generally. You work with the same people—surgeons, techs, nurses—for years, and it's tense sometimes, but we wisecrack. Still, you know, if I'm mad enough, I'll talk some about what has happened. I know I shouldn't. I've been scolded. But hell, sometimes you have to say, even if it gets around."

I admire the nurse's loyalty. I also admire what I take to be her courageous indiscretions, confidences—perhaps made in intensive care to Dr. Smith, perhaps whispered to other nurses, in fury, in the recovery room, right after some bumbling procedure. She also feels loyal to patients.

The basic fact seems extraordinary on the face of it: There's no dependable way that referring physicians can accurately judge the ability of surgeons. Those who are in the know feel they can't come out and say. Perhaps their indiscretions keep the system honest enough so that it usually works in spite of itself. Certainly nothing more formal helps out.

Records of procedures are of little help in judging surgical quality. They aren't routinely available to referring physicians for scrutiny. And even were they, they record results that defy quantification—some surgeons who operate skillfully on the

200

sickest patients have poor complication and survival rates. Others, who stumble through unnecessary procedures on nearly well patients, have fine-looking statistics. Sometimes the best short-stops in baseball make the most errors. They come close to making plays others wouldn't even try.

Members of hospital tissue review committees, who check on most surgery that results in the removal of normal tissue and tissue indicating unanticipated problems, do become aware of who performs flagrant numbers of unnecessary procedures. They may eventually scold the offender, and inform the chief of surgery. And chart reviews of individual surgeons' work are undertaken by hospitals, but only when long-recalcitrant practitioners resist more tactful pressures to reform.

Surgeons' rights to entrepreneurial independence, and to the autonomous control of patients' treatment, are well protected by custom and by law. The professional societies representing most of the surgical specialties have frequently resisted even such mild controls on the art of their members as issuing protocols suggesting which sets of symptoms ought to lead to which procedures.

The key issue of referrals goes beyond supplying knowledgeable recommendations to sick patients in search of surgery. It leads right to the adequacy of quality control in surgery. If no one is free to examine or to speak of the quality of surgeons, even within the profession, who is minding the gates? Who guards patients' well-being against whatever misfits slip through and start careers as poor surgeons? And what happens at the other end? Who guards patients from the occasional surgeon whose quality of performance suddenly slides because of illness, alcohol, emotional problems, or—most commonly—advancing age?

The medical official most likely to become aware of the terminal cases of surgical negligence is the coroner. I seek out a "coroner's coroner," Michael Baden, formerly chief medical examiner of New York City, and ask him (over sliced steak and broccoli, served on a kitchen table full of famous people's autopsy photographs) to estimate his ability to function as a guardian

201

of surgical quality, at least in the most extreme cases he must encounter. He is a looming man, large, quick-gestured, volatile, and candid.

"I am just where you'd look to find a gatekeeper—but there is no gatekeeper on surgical quality," he says. "I see the most amazing cases. I can't claim to have much effect. Well, I have, but only in one or two specific *outrageous* cases. Even then, the question of blame for procedures-gone-wrong gets so complex and so legally difficult that actions you might assume would be simple for me to take turn out to be all but impossible. These guys can sue you.

"I'll tell you a story. A young girl was brought to the morgue some years back. She was Puerto Rican. She had had a heart problem. A certain surgeon put an artificial heart valve in the girl—she needed one—but his treatment had killed her. He had put it in backwards, sewed it in so when it should have opened to the flow of blood, it had blocked it instead.

"How do you judge that? Perhaps in the chaos of some emergency in the surgery, that moment of confusion was easy to understand. Perhaps it might have occurred to any surgeon. At any rate, I did the autopsy, and I identified the cause of death. My assignment under the law is to discover and report on all cases of 'unnatural death.' There was some skirmishing about what to fill out on the death certificate here—you can imagine. Finally, what went onto the certificate was, 'Cause of death: inverted mitral valve prosthesis.' It was enough to help protect the surgeon. The victim's parents spoke English poorly, and they were poor. Even if they had known that they could request a copy of the death certificate, how would they understand that medical jargon to mean someone might have made a surgical error? Years later, I mentioned the case—no names—in a talk before some surgeons. The rumor mill operated, and the next time I saw that surgeon he was mad at me for mentioning it. There is no gatekeeper on surgical quality."

In fact, there are some gatekeepers of surgical quality. A choice of surgeon made by spinning about three times and sticking a pin in the yellow pages entries (giving equal odds of choos-

202

ing Goode, or St. James, or Stearne) would probably yield a competent surgeon. There are gross controls on who operates, although no one within the medical system can, at any moment, claim to know who does fair work, usually, and who does fine work, almost always.

Medical school is hard to get into, which means that dullards and underachievers seldom become doctors. That helps some, but also causes some further problems with quality. Michael Baden (who, in addition to being a coroner, is on the admissions committee of a major medical school) says that "the feat of being accepted for admission requires such single-mindedness, manipulativeness, and skill at self-advancement that no one should be surprised when most doctors turn out single-minded, manipulative, and skillfully self-advancing."

Beyond that, board certification by the various Boards of Surgeons is rigorous, so that it's not uncommon to hear of practicing surgeons who fail, or who qualify only on their second or third attempt.

Besides that, the mechanisms of self-policing—even if followed no more dutifully by doctors than by those in other wealthy, large, controversial industries—do often work. They work slowly, and sometimes haphazardly, and let unfortunate events slip past that could have been halted, but they often seem sooner or later to work. Most self-policing controls only local jurisdictions—it takes place on the level of hospital review committees, or county or state medical committees—and its effects go no further than that. Duds are most often moved on, and can repeat their fumbling elsewhere.

And while the poor surgeons are on location, their colleagues, at least, do grow more aware of them. Within the limits of institutional protocols, colleagues do try to oversee likely occasions of bad surgery. They make critical comments. They drop in to the operating room to see what's going on. They whisper, and warn off their special pals, to the limits of liability. Reputations slacken and the resulting poor business may be enough to drive a substandard practitioner away.

Active surgeons concerned with such issues spend most of

that concern on one sort of quality control problem: respected, even grand, old men recently gone sour. Stories abound. Nearly every hospital has had its version of the dilemma. Such problems are not the stuff of unrestrained journalism; one must trade tact in return for frankness.

Some well-established, recently sound, aging gentlemen, with fine reputations, solid records, established connections—and now failing health or habits—cannot bring themselves to quit. Physical decline, alcoholism, emotional problems may have dulled judgment and technical skill. The profession calls them "impaired physicians" and state medical societies have standing committees to study the subject. Impaired physicians, once noticed, are leaned on, their practices curtailed and overseen—tactfully, if possible, and strenuously only as a last resort. The long process of containing them starts with discreet gossip by dismayed colleagues. In one hospital a senior man was said to be taking hours to do half-hour procedures, and seemed to be getting lost in the middle of elementary anatomical excursions, and just the other day he was bailed out by so-and-so, a passing colleague, and didn't even seem to know it. Experienced nurses, mid-operation, utter reminders tactfully. Elsewhere, another, unnamed, man was rumored to have worked despite occasional petit-mal seizures during operations. And still another was remembered for a final year of operating under the influence of Scotch whisky.

Such stories, while memorable (every surgeon I asked conceded that he could speak of such situations), are also rare—describing few of the hundred thousand surgeons. They are important, not as a warning off for prospective patients but because they demonstrate something about surgeons' basic collective priorities. In the cases I heard about—perhaps half a dozen described, and a few more mentioned—matters were handled tactfully, even though with each passing day a few patients faced unusual risks. Meanwhile, failing colleagues were "spoken to" over golf or beer, and urged firmly to retire. In one case, when a failing surgeon was scheduled to have the physical examination mandatory for his annual hospital recertification, the doctor who was to administer it was approached by concerned colleagues; the problem surgeon sidestepped the diplomatic effort by having the examination in a distant city, where it was performed by an old friend. Decorum was maintained, but the tactful pressure had failed. He stayed on a while longer.

The principle of professional autonomy was preserved, even in those instances that must have made some conscientious practitioners feel compromised, and perhaps that's the point. Surgeons do well in their careers. They make money, enjoy high status, and feel useful, even crucial. The very rules that they have set up to protect their freedom to do as they see fit are responsible for their quality control problems. The problem is therefore stubborn, built into the foundations of surgeons' work structure: The measures that would make the system respond less sluggishly to incompetents are largely taboo. They turn out to be exactly the measures that threaten to curtail every surgeon's independence.

If surgeons were salaried, and not fee-for-service practitioners, whoever paid them would no doubt evaluate performance. As things stand, most have no employers to let them go when they slack off.

Were there expert outside reevaluators, such as the examiners who occasionally fly along with pilots, surgical quality could be subject to periodic formal scrutiny.

Were records independently constructed and open freely to colleagues, the truths of the surgical corridor might be more widely circulated. Were there (to pursue the pilot analogy) a device like a flight recorder in every operating room—say an always-running video camera and microphone—private events might be publicly reconstructed if need arose.

Were there patient advocates participating in postsurgical tissue review and morbidity conferences at hospitals, poor surgeons might come under pressure sooner.

There are indeed drawbacks to all these hedgings of power. They invade privacy, create stress for the surgeon in the OR, where cool heads are needed, and build pressure for the most complete and conservative treatment in every case. Such changes in the nature of surgical oversight seem highly unlikely soon. But versions of such mechanisms do operate—in mild doses that (while only mildly effective) leave doctors' autonomy intact.

HMOs do provide salaried or contract surgeons and, as employers of sorts, do supervise quality some. The county medical society will supply lists of surgeons, although not judgments of quality. If they leave certain names out, that mercy is done by tactful secretaries. There are performance review mechanisms—the discreet standing hospital committees whose power is largely informal. They are empowered to the degree that they must be to address the worst offenders. Beyond that, one is cautioned, medicine's an art; let it be. Surgeons accept and participate in this benign oversight machinery; it is partly effective, and partly reassuring. It works to mitigate the worst cases, eventually but not quickly, locally but not widely, and discreetly, not forthrightly. It protects surgeons' art, and surgeons' business.

"The same difficulties that prevent you from continuing to practice effectively also prevent you from knowing that it's time to quit," Russell Stearne says. We are discussing impaired physicians. He is on his way to work. He is well-rested, relaxed, unimpaired. "How incompetent do you have to be before the rest of the medical community calls you on it? That's a tough one, a gray area. Should any surgeon not as competent as me quit operating? Should I quit because I'm not Denton Cooley?"

"Is he better than you?"

"Oh, he's pretty good. Surgical competence isn't really just about technique. An intelligent ape could be trained to cut and sew. The most important thing about competence is actually judgment, and to tell the truth, the one thing you can't judge for yourself is your judgment. That's where the problem of impaired physicians who won't quit comes from. When your judgment goes, how can you know? I wouldn't do any better than anyone else in telling that. I say I'll retire by sixty. I hope I do. Then again, maybe I'll go out and sell my soul to the devil so I never grow old."

Stearne is ambling through the hospital's long corridors, eyeing the competition, returning quips and curt nods from other physicians. He's on his way to surgery, to perform an operation that is moderately elective—anytime in the next week will probably do. It will help the patient for a while, but not for long. The patient's prognosis, Stearne says, is moderately poor. His foot has gone blotchy from occluded circulation. His attitude is moderately resigned—in Stearne's office yesterday he didn't seem to care much about what happened next. This will be his fourth, and most likely his last, bout of limb-saving vascular surgery. We encounter the patient now, parked on a cart by the elevators in the blind end of a hallway, accompanied by an orderly.

"Herbert," Stearne shouts at the half-dozing man on the cart, "I'm going to have a look at some pictures of you—the ones we took before in X-ray. Then I'll see you in the operating room. Don't worry." The patient nods agreement without opening his eyes. The elevator door slides open and the orderly trundles Herbert aboard.

Stearne continues up the corridor into the X-ray department, to collect shots of the occluded artery. "A walking disaster case," he mutters.

The radiologist sits in this small chamber all day, lanky and black-haired, attending to ghostly pictures relentlessly and methodically. She recites a checklist to herself as she inspects each photograph. She says this wards off the carelessness of long habit. Radiologists' rooms are always like inside cabins of ships, cavelike and yet set in the midst of hospitals' traffic flow. She peers into lungs and limbs, reconstructing three-dimensional trouble from anatomical shadows in two dimensions. All day, she whispers about what's wrong, leaning into a small microphone cupped in her palm. Visitors interrupt constantly. She glances at Stearne now, nods recognition, and presses a black button built into her worktable. X-rays on a rack flip in sequence past the viewing screen above her. Ten patients' troubles flash by.

She stops at the hip, the femur, the knee, of the walking

disaster case and offers Stearne some vigorous medical metaphors. "He has a real pruned tree." Her hand waves over an area of shadow where there should be a florid branching of vessels; only a few thin ones wander, branchless. "His arborization is crappy," she says. To the radiologist, either vascular repair or amputation seems clearly necessary. She adds rodent insult to vegetable injury: with her finger she traces the popliteal artery; it thickens and thins with plaque on its trail down the thigh to a final clog. "It's a very ratty vessel," she says. Stearne picks up the X-rays and steps out into daylight for just a moment, then down, down into surgery.

In the dressing room, Stearne acts unusually cordial. He throws me a blouse and pants from the shelves of clean green operating room clothing. I dress. We walk down the hall toward the operating room, and meet Stearne's partner, Culver. "Look at this man," says Stearne, pointing at me. "I deliberately gave him an outfit that was far too large for him, so he'd look funny."

Unlike radiologists' caves, where hidden territory is revealed only to knowing eyes, operating rooms have windows. They face inward, on to corridors full of passing surgical staff. There are no secrets within this secret place. The stainless steel scrub sinks in the hall overlook a choice of two operations in adjacent rooms. Surgeons putting in their ten minutes of ablution keep entertained and up to date on colleagues' performances, joking with each other and studying hovering figures at work beyond the glass.

Stearne turns on hot water, stares into the operating room through the window, and scrubs hard. Herbert lies in there stoned out on Pentothal. Stearne watches as the staff works and chats inside. The discreet anesthesiologist stabs Herbert's spine with a thick needle, paralyzing and numbing the legs. Two nurses lay green tables of silver tongs, pliers, tweezers, knives, scissors, small hoes, and also tubing, both transparent and opaque. Things go on here, too, in spite of the windows. As I wander in, the nurses' and technicians' discussion smacks of sacrilege. Secrets are being discussed. A doctor working across the corridor, says a nurse, is taking three hours to do a twenty-minute job he's never done before. Next topic.

"The girl that arrested here last week—the kid?"

"She died. Thursday."

"Probably best thing could happen—brain damage is what I heard."

"Let's not discuss it. There shouldn't be a discussion here, understand?" The nurses all look at me.

Through the window I see that Culver has joined Stearne at the scrub sink. Culver winks as the nurses glance past me toward the window.

Stearne comes in, receives gloves, checks preparations, and shouts Herbert alert. He's a stone-faced old man, with cauliflower ears, nose, brows, chin. In aquamarine paper beret, he resembles an old pope, eyes closed in prayer, lips pursed in concentration. He's gathering strength. Never opening his eyes, he says, "I didn't get to sleep until two A.M."

"We didn't want you to sleep all night. You're going to sleep all day," Stearne says to him cheerfully. He finishes the orange paint job the nurses have begun on Herbert's numb legs. The anesthesiologist sets up a cloth screen a foot high across Herbert's neck, making two worlds. Herbert above. Herbert's body below.

I look across the room, out through the windows and down the length of the surgical corridor. No one in view. When I look back, Stearne has already made four diagonal slashes, each a few red inches long, deep, nearly bloodless, at intervals along the inside of the right thigh. Stearne sets about freeing what he calls "God's gift to us—the saphenous vein." It makes a straight run up from heel to the joining of leg and belly.

That homely, vigorous language of the radiologist shows again, returned to vegetable themes now. Stearne says he is "harvesting" the saphenous vein. He labors at the reaping. The vein begins to peel out intact, made of strong tissue, and wide enough to be useful in this operation. Stearne disconnects it from its roots, tying each tributary off in turn with black sutures, and inch by inch, threads the freed vessel back from slit to slit. At knee level, with nearly two feet of saphenous vein dangling free, he's got enough.

He opens and deepens a cleft directly under the arched meeting of upper and lower leg bones, in the depths of flesh below the knee joint. He ties off the saphenous vein, leaving its unneeded lower end behind. The freed section of the vein wanders out from this cave like a thin snake. He severs it from the body, carries it across the room to a green-topped workbench. He cleans the outside of clinging scraps, pumps it full of saline with a hypodermic, watches for leaks, closes up the few he finds with tiny stitches, then brings the vein back to the patient.

It's to be installed upside down now, so the vein's valve flaps—which have prevented the column of returning blood within the leg from falling back down between heartbeats— won't block the flow of blood on the vessel's new arterial mission. Stearne decides, for some reason, to chat up the patient again. Herbert dozes, not quite out cold, up at the top end of the table, keeping company with the anesthesiologist.

"Herbert, what's wrong with your leg that brought you here?" Stearne shouts. Herbert opens his eyes now. They're luminous, ocean blue.

"Pain," he mumbles, and closes his eyes again.

Stearne reenters the cave under the knee, and dissects still further inward until he finds the popliteal artery. It's pale, as thick as a fountain pen, and seems to deserve Stearne's praise.

"This is soft and rubbery to here. Seems very good—I'm going up a little more." He slices upward toward the hip a few inches further. "Here's the occlusion. Very well defined. Just like that X-ray." He points. "We'll come in just past it."

To come in just past it, he will control blood flow to and from the chosen point, clamping off a section of popliteal artery. He will puncture the isolated section of artery. He will spread the puncture into an oblate slit. He will shape the slit so it will kiss, mouth to mouth, the end of the freed saphenous vein, for the rest of the patient's life. This kiss is the reason for the surgery. It's the opening of a new blood route, a way, for a while, around the pain.

Stearne's stitches are tiny. Stearne calls for a new instrument: "That pair of Dr. Boswell's glasses. I need 'em."

The circulating nurse, a willowy and fast-moving person about whom Stearne has said, "Lifts weights—she's a body builder," slips onto the surgeon's nose a pair of scholar's black-framed spectacles. Upon their lenses are glued small, dice-shaped magnifying blocks. Stearne's face moves slowly downward, like an antiaircraft gun shortening range, raking the length of her body. In a thin, robotic voice, Stearne says, "I can see right through your clothing now."

The nurse laughs a laugh that says Stearne's acting up again, and she goes about her business. Stearne turns back to the cave, looking through Dr. Boswell's glasses. He sews, and eventually says, "Through these glasses, this vein looks like a garden hose, and these big fat fingers get in the way."

Then he moves up to the soft tarpaulin of skin that spans the triangle of navel, pubic mound, and hip. He makes a new incision, and again dissects inward, again stitches closed bleeding vessels. He's heading for the profunda femoris, to be the site of the upper anastomosis, a second kiss, and the source of new leg blood. In the midst of his search he glances up and smiles at the aging nurse to his left, who is pinned in place by her obligation to hold on to retractors that stretch this new incision.

"You all right, Charlene?"

"Yeah."

"Charlene thinks she's all right." No one laughs.

Stearne finds the artery, clears around it, chases it up through a hardened patch. "He's got a very tight profunda block," he announces, "and I'm going to do an endarterectomy." An operation within an operation. He does what is required. He clamps the profunda femoris, fore and aft, ties tributaries, hauls Teflon ties closed to seal the area, and unzips the sidewall, revealing a two-inch run of plaque. He flays the vessel open, spreads it like the belly of a dissected frog. The plaque is

211

white as soapstone this time, and the shape of an arrowhead. He slips the point of a tongs underneath, and works the plaque's edge free of the intima, the artery's inner wall. It comes away, for the most part, in one teaspoon-sized section. "That'll make a tremendous difference in flow," he says.

As he works, deepening, positioning, sewing, taking away, he accumulates scrap. Charlene collects it in containers, for the lab, where pathologists will examine the tissue under microscopes. As Stearne pulls used sops from the wounds, the circulating nurse lays them out, each one a yard long and a hand's width wide, blotched with blood, side by side on a green towel on the floor. She lines up a dozen, and suddenly they resemble bacon on a green griddle. The aspirator sucks blood and saline rinse halfway across the room through transparent tubing to a jug by the far wall; the suction sounds like bacon frying. I recall breakfasts with the surgical staff. Stearne calls for mosquito clamps and bulldog clamps. Time speeds.

The geography of the jungle cleft grows familiar, cliff of fat above red corrugated muscle floor. It becomes the only world, where all events take place, more real to us than the life out through the windows, where people laugh and, once, someone calls something out, just beyond intelligibility.

As he stitches, Stearne begins speaking of his new puppy. "She jumps in bed at three A.M., loves snuggling. She discovers the cat asleep at the end of the bed, and flies off the bed, chasing it downstairs. The other cat, who sleeps down there, hears this. The downstairs cat hates the upstairs cat and runs out to meet it. Lots of hissing results."

He calls for the weightlifter: "Remove Dr. Boswell's glasses." He halts her as she reaches for them. "One last look," he says. He rakes her with them again. Then they get taken.

He is disturbed. He asks slowly, in a voice that sounds full of wonder, "Why does the surgical lamp keep moving?"

"It's like the sun, moves slowly across the sky," Culver says.

Stearne begins sewing together the subfascia of fat.

Nurses commence sponge count in canon. "One, two ('One'), three ('two'), four ('three') . . ."

The patient stirs. Culver dances past the table, heading for the outside world. "Another cure! O happy feet!" he cries, and exits, then waves back in through the window.

Stearne fires off long rows of stainless staples along the incision lines—zippers where mayhem just showed. Off drip, the patient whispers a question that comes right to the point:

"Is this going to take the pain away?"

"I've done the best I can," Stearne says.